50 Duck Recipes for Home

By: Kelly Johnson

Table of Contents

- Roast Duck with Orange Glaze
- Peking Duck Pancakes
- Duck Confit
- Duck à l'Orange
- Crispy Duck Tacos
- Asian-Inspired Duck Stir-Fry
- Duck and Wild Mushroom Risotto
- Spicy Mango Duck Salad
- Honey-Glazed Duck Breast
- Smoked Duck Breast with Raspberry Sauce
- Grilled Duck Skewers with Plum Sauce
- Duck Gumbo
- Duck and Black Bean Enchiladas
- Duck and Cherry Sauce
- Duck Spring Rolls
- Teriyaki Duck Noodles
- Duck and Cranberry Stuffed Acorn Squash
- Thai Red Curry Duck
- Citrus-Marinated Grilled Duck
- Duck and Fig Pizza
- Hoisin-Glazed Duck Wings
- Mediterranean Duck Salad
- Duck Liver Pâté
- Moroccan Spiced Duck Tagine
- Duck and Blueberry Balsamic Reduction
- Duck Sausage and Apple-Stuffed Squash
- Duck and Port Wine Reduction
- Spicy Cajun Duck Pasta
- Duck Ravioli with Sage Brown Butter
- Duck and Pineapple Skewers
- Sesame-Crusted Duck Breast
- Duck and Roasted Beet Salad
- Duck and Apricot Compote
- Duck Ramen Bowl
- Orange-Chipotle Glazed Duck Drumsticks

- Duck and Sweet Potato Hash
- Duck and Mango Salsa
- Duck and Spinach Stuffed Shells
- Five-Spice Duck Lettuce Wraps
- Duck and Blue Cheese Flatbread
- Duck and Cranberry Puff Pastry Bites
- Duck and Asparagus Quiche
- BBQ Pulled Duck Sliders
- Duck and Roasted Garlic Mashed Potatoes
- Duck and Lemon Risotto
- Duck and Portobello Mushroom Pizza
- Smoked Duck and Gouda Quesadillas
- Duck and Caramelized Onion Tart
- Duck and Apple Slaw
- Ginger-Soy Glazed Duck Breast

Roast Duck with Orange Glaze

Ingredients:

For the Duck:

- 1 whole duck (about 4-5 pounds)
- Salt and pepper, to taste
- 1 tablespoon olive oil

For the Orange Glaze:

- 1 cup orange juice
- Zest of one orange
- 1/4 cup soy sauce
- 1/4 cup honey
- 2 tablespoons rice vinegar
- 1 teaspoon grated ginger
- 2 cloves garlic, minced
- 1 tablespoon cornstarch (optional, for thickening)

Instructions:

Preheat the Oven:
- Preheat your oven to 375°F (190°C).

Prepare the Duck:
- Rinse the duck inside and out, and pat it dry with paper towels.
- Season the duck with salt and pepper, both inside and outside.
- Place the duck on a roasting rack set in a roasting pan.

Score the Duck Skin:
- Use a sharp knife to score the duck skin in a crisscross pattern. This helps the fat render and the skin to become crispy.

Roast the Duck:
- Roast the duck in the preheated oven for about 2 to 2.5 hours, or until the internal temperature reaches 165°F (74°C) and the skin is golden brown and crispy.

Prepare the Orange Glaze:
- In a saucepan, combine orange juice, orange zest, soy sauce, honey, rice vinegar, ginger, and garlic.

- Bring the mixture to a simmer over medium heat and let it cook for about 10-15 minutes until it thickens slightly.
- If you prefer a thicker glaze, mix 1 tablespoon of cornstarch with a little water to create a slurry and stir it into the glaze. Cook for an additional 2-3 minutes until thickened.

Glaze the Duck:
- Brush the orange glaze over the duck during the last 20-30 minutes of roasting, ensuring a glossy finish.

Rest and Serve:
- Once the duck reaches the desired temperature, remove it from the oven and let it rest for 10-15 minutes before carving.
- Serve the roast duck slices drizzled with any remaining orange glaze.

Enjoy your delicious Roast Duck with Orange Glaze!

Peking Duck Pancakes

Ingredients:

For the Peking Duck:

- 1 whole duck (about 5-6 pounds)
- 2 tablespoons honey
- 2 tablespoons soy sauce
- 2 tablespoons hoisin sauce
- 1 tablespoon rice vinegar
- 1 teaspoon sesame oil
- 1 teaspoon Chinese five-spice powder
- 4 green onions, sliced
- 1 cucumber, julienned
- Hoisin sauce, for serving
- Mandarin pancakes (store-bought or homemade, see below)

For the Mandarin Pancakes:

- 2 cups all-purpose flour
- 3/4 cup boiling water
- 1 tablespoon sesame oil

Instructions:

For the Mandarin Pancakes:

Prepare the Dough:
- In a large bowl, gradually add boiling water to the flour, stirring continuously until a dough forms.
- Knead the dough on a floured surface until smooth, cover with a damp cloth, and let it rest for 30 minutes.

Shape the Pancakes:
- Roll the dough into a log shape and cut it into 16 equal pieces.
- Roll each piece into a small ball and flatten it into a thin pancake shape (about 3 inches in diameter).
- Brush each pancake with sesame oil.

Cook the Pancakes:
- Heat a non-stick skillet over medium-high heat.
- Cook each pancake for about 1-2 minutes on each side until they puff up and have a golden brown color.

- Keep the cooked pancakes warm by covering them with a clean cloth.

For the Peking Duck:

Preheat the Oven:
- Preheat your oven to 375°F (190°C).

Prepare the Duck:
- Rinse the duck inside and out, and pat it dry with paper towels.
- Combine honey, soy sauce, hoisin sauce, rice vinegar, sesame oil, and Chinese five-spice powder in a bowl to make the marinade.

Marinate the Duck:
- Brush the duck with the marinade inside and out.
- Let the duck marinate for at least 1-2 hours or overnight in the refrigerator.

Roast the Duck:
- Place the duck on a rack in a roasting pan and roast in the preheated oven for about 2 to 2.5 hours, or until the skin is crispy and the internal temperature reaches 165°F (74°C).

Slice the Duck:
- Once the duck is cooked, let it rest for a few minutes, and then carve it into thin slices.

Assemble the Pancakes:
- Spread a small amount of hoisin sauce on each pancake.
- Place a few slices of duck, green onions, and julienned cucumber on each pancake.
- Roll up the pancake and secure it with a toothpick if needed.

Serve your Peking Duck Pancakes while they are warm. Enjoy this delightful Chinese dish!

Duck Confit

Ingredients:

For the Duck Confit:

- 4 duck leg quarters
- Salt and freshly ground black pepper
- 4 cloves garlic, minced
- 4 sprigs fresh thyme
- 2 bay leaves
- Duck fat (enough to submerge the duck legs)

For Serving:

- Mashed potatoes or crusty bread
- Fresh parsley, chopped (for garnish)

Instructions:

Prep the Duck Legs:
- Pat the duck legs dry with paper towels.
- Generously season each duck leg with salt and freshly ground black pepper.

Seasoning:
- Rub each duck leg with minced garlic, ensuring an even distribution.
- Place a sprig of thyme on each leg and add a bay leaf.

Confit Process:
- In a large, oven-safe dish, arrange the seasoned duck legs in a single layer.
- Melt duck fat in a saucepan until it's completely liquid, then pour enough over the duck legs to submerge them.

Cooking:
- Preheat your oven to 200°F (93°C).
- Cover the dish with a lid or aluminum foil and place it in the preheated oven for about 6-8 hours, or until the duck is very tender and falls off the bone.

Cooling and Storing:
- Allow the duck to cool in the fat until it reaches room temperature.
- Once cooled, you can store the duck legs in the fat in an airtight container in the refrigerator for an extended period.

Reheating and Crisping:

- When ready to serve, preheat the oven to a higher temperature, around 400°F (200°C).
- Remove the duck legs from the fat and place them on a baking sheet.
- Roast in the hot oven for 15-20 minutes or until the skin becomes crispy.

Serve:
- Serve the Duck Confit on a bed of mashed potatoes or with crusty bread.
- Garnish with freshly chopped parsley for a burst of freshness.

Enjoy this rich and flavorful Duck Confit!

Duck à l'Orange

Ingredients:

For the Duck:

- 2 duck breasts, skin-on
- Salt and black pepper, to taste

For the Orange Sauce:

- 1 cup orange juice
- Zest of one orange
- 1/2 cup chicken broth
- 1/4 cup red wine vinegar
- 1/4 cup honey
- 2 tablespoons Grand Marnier or Cointreau (orange liqueur)
- 2 tablespoons unsalted butter
- Salt and black pepper, to taste

For Garnish:

- Orange slices
- Fresh parsley, chopped

Instructions:

Prepare the Duck:
- Score the duck skin with a sharp knife in a crosshatch pattern. Season both sides with salt and black pepper.

Sear the Duck:
- Heat a large skillet over medium-high heat. Place the duck breasts, skin side down, in the skillet. Sear for about 5-7 minutes, until the skin is golden and crispy. Flip and sear for an additional 2-3 minutes.

Finish Cooking in the Oven:
- Preheat the oven to 375°F (190°C).
- Transfer the duck breasts to a baking dish and finish cooking in the preheated oven for about 12-15 minutes or until the internal temperature reaches 145°F (63°C) for medium-rare or 160°F (71°C) for medium.

Make the Orange Sauce:

- In the same skillet, combine orange juice, orange zest, chicken broth, red wine vinegar, honey, and orange liqueur. Bring to a simmer and let it reduce by half.

Finish the Sauce:
- Whisk in the butter until the sauce is glossy and smooth. Season with salt and black pepper to taste.

Slice and Serve:
- Let the duck breasts rest for a few minutes before slicing them into thin strips.
- Serve the sliced duck on a plate, drizzle with the orange sauce, and garnish with orange slices and chopped fresh parsley.

Optional: Side Dish Suggestions
- Duck à l'Orange pairs well with roasted vegetables, mashed potatoes, or a simple green salad.

Enjoy your delicious Duck à l'Orange!

Crispy Duck Tacos

Ingredients:

For the Crispy Duck:

- 2 duck breasts, skin-on
- Salt and black pepper, to taste
- 1 tablespoon Chinese five-spice powder
- 2 tablespoons soy sauce
- 2 tablespoons hoisin sauce
- 2 tablespoons honey
- 1 tablespoon sesame oil

For the Tacos:

- Small taco-sized tortillas (corn or flour)
- Shredded red cabbage
- Sliced green onions
- Fresh cilantro leaves
- Lime wedges

Instructions:

Prepare the Duck:
- Preheat your oven to 375°F (190°C).
- Score the duck skin in a crosshatch pattern, being careful not to cut into the meat.
- Season both sides of the duck breasts with salt, black pepper, and Chinese five-spice powder.

Marinate the Duck:
- In a small bowl, mix soy sauce, hoisin sauce, honey, and sesame oil.
- Brush the duck breasts with the marinade, ensuring they are well coated.
- Let the duck marinate for at least 30 minutes to allow the flavors to infuse.

Sear and Roast the Duck:
- Heat an oven-safe skillet over medium-high heat. Place the duck breasts, skin side down, and sear for about 3-4 minutes until the skin is crispy.
- Flip the duck breasts and transfer the skillet to the preheated oven. Roast for 10-12 minutes or until the internal temperature reaches 145°F (63°C) for medium-rare.

Rest and Slice:
- Allow the duck breasts to rest for a few minutes before slicing them thinly.

Assemble the Tacos:
- Warm the tortillas in a dry skillet or microwave.
- Place slices of crispy duck on each tortilla.
- Top with shredded red cabbage, sliced green onions, and fresh cilantro leaves.

Serve with Lime Wedges:
- Serve the Crispy Duck Tacos with lime wedges on the side for a burst of citrusy flavor.

Feel free to customize the tacos with additional toppings like sliced radishes, avocado, or your favorite hot sauce. Enjoy your Crispy Duck Tacos!

Asian-Inspired Duck Stir-Fry

Ingredients:

For the Crispy Duck:

- 2 duck breasts, skin-on
- Salt and black pepper, to taste
- 1 teaspoon Chinese five-spice powder
- Flour tortillas

For the Slaw:

- 2 cups shredded Napa cabbage
- 1 carrot, julienned
- 1/4 cup chopped cilantro
- 2 tablespoons rice vinegar
- 1 tablespoon soy sauce
- 1 tablespoon honey
- 1 tablespoon sesame oil

For the Hoisin Sauce:

- 1/4 cup hoisin sauce
- 2 tablespoons soy sauce
- 1 tablespoon honey
- 1 teaspoon Sriracha (optional for heat)

Instructions:

Prepare the Duck:
- Score the duck skin with a sharp knife and season with salt, black pepper, and Chinese five-spice powder.
- In a hot skillet, sear the duck breasts, skin side down, until crispy. Flip and cook until desired doneness.
- Let the duck rest before slicing it into thin strips.

Make the Slaw:
- In a bowl, combine shredded Napa cabbage, julienned carrot, cilantro, rice vinegar, soy sauce, honey, and sesame oil. Toss to combine.

Prepare the Hoisin Sauce:

- In a small bowl, mix hoisin sauce, soy sauce, honey, and Sriracha. Adjust the sweetness and spiciness to your liking.

Assemble the Tacos:
- Warm the flour tortillas.
- Spread a spoonful of hoisin sauce on each tortilla.
- Add a layer of the slaw, followed by slices of crispy duck.
- Drizzle with additional hoisin sauce if desired.
- Garnish with extra cilantro and serve.

Asian-Inspired Duck Stir-Fry

Ingredients:

- 2 duck breasts, thinly sliced
- 2 tablespoons soy sauce
- 1 tablespoon oyster sauce
- 1 tablespoon hoisin sauce
- 1 tablespoon rice vinegar
- 1 tablespoon sesame oil
- 1 tablespoon vegetable oil
- 2 garlic cloves, minced
- 1 tablespoon fresh ginger, grated
- 1 red bell pepper, thinly sliced
- 1 carrot, julienned
- 1 cup snap peas, trimmed
- Cooked rice or noodles, for serving
- Green onions and sesame seeds for garnish

Instructions:

Marinate the Duck:
- In a bowl, combine sliced duck with soy sauce, oyster sauce, hoisin sauce, and rice vinegar. Let it marinate for at least 15 minutes.

Stir-Fry the Duck:
- Heat vegetable oil and sesame oil in a wok or large skillet over high heat.
- Add minced garlic and grated ginger, stir-frying for about 30 seconds until fragrant.
- Add the marinated duck slices and cook until browned and cooked through. Remove from the wok and set aside.

Stir-Fry Vegetables:
- In the same wok, add a bit more oil if needed. Stir-fry red bell pepper, julienned carrot, and snap peas until they are crisp-tender.

Combine and Serve:
- Return the cooked duck to the wok and toss everything together until well combined.
- Serve the duck stir-fry over cooked rice or noodles.
- Garnish with sliced green onions and sesame seeds.

Enjoy your Crispy Duck Tacos and Asian-Inspired Duck Stir-Fry!

Duck and Wild Mushroom Risotto

Ingredients:

For the Duck:

- 2 duck breasts, skin-on
- Salt and black pepper, to taste
- 1 tablespoon olive oil

For the Risotto:

- 1 cup Arborio rice
- 1/2 cup dry white wine
- 4 cups chicken or vegetable broth, kept warm
- 1 cup mixed wild mushrooms (such as shiitake, oyster, and cremini), sliced
- 1 small onion, finely chopped
- 2 cloves garlic, minced
- 1/2 cup Parmesan cheese, grated
- 2 tablespoons unsalted butter
- Fresh thyme leaves, for garnish
- Salt and black pepper, to taste

Instructions:

For the Duck:

    Preheat Oven:
- Preheat your oven to 400°F (200°C).

    Prepare the Duck:
- Score the duck skin with a sharp knife and season with salt and black pepper.
- Heat olive oil in an oven-safe skillet over medium-high heat.
- Sear the duck breasts, skin side down, until golden brown. Flip and sear the other side for a few minutes.
- Transfer the skillet to the preheated oven and roast for about 10-15 minutes or until the duck reaches your desired doneness.
- Remove from the oven, let it rest for a few minutes, then slice the duck into thin strips.

For the Risotto:

Sauté Mushrooms:
- In a separate large skillet or wide saucepan, heat a tablespoon of butter over medium heat.
- Add chopped onions and garlic, sauté until softened.
- Add the mixed wild mushrooms and cook until they release their moisture and become golden brown.

Cook the Rice:
- Stir in Arborio rice and cook for a couple of minutes until the rice is lightly toasted.
- Pour in the white wine and stir until it's mostly absorbed.

Add Broth:
- Begin adding the warm broth, one ladle at a time, stirring frequently. Allow each ladle to be absorbed before adding the next.

Finish the Risotto:
- Continue this process until the rice is creamy and cooked to al dente, which should take about 18-20 minutes.
- Stir in grated Parmesan cheese and the remaining butter. Season with salt and black pepper to taste.

Serve:
- Spoon the risotto onto plates or into bowls.
- Top each serving with sliced duck breast.
- Garnish with fresh thyme leaves and additional Parmesan if desired.

Enjoy your Duck and Wild Mushroom Risotto!

Spicy Mango Duck Salad

Ingredients:

For the Duck:

- 2 duck breasts, skin-on
- Salt and black pepper, to taste
- 1 teaspoon ground cumin
- 1 teaspoon paprika
- 1 teaspoon chili powder

For the Salad:

- 1 large ripe mango, peeled, pitted, and diced
- 1 red bell pepper, thinly sliced
- 1 cucumber, thinly sliced
- 1 cup cherry tomatoes, halved
- 1/4 cup red onion, thinly sliced
- 1/4 cup fresh cilantro, chopped

For the Dressing:

- 2 tablespoons olive oil
- 1 tablespoon soy sauce
- 1 tablespoon honey
- 1 tablespoon lime juice
- 1 teaspoon sriracha (adjust to taste)

Instructions:

For the Duck:

    Preheat Oven:
- Preheat your oven to 400°F (200°C).

    Prepare the Duck:
- Score the duck skin with a sharp knife and season with salt, black pepper, cumin, paprika, and chili powder.
- Heat an oven-safe skillet over medium-high heat. Place the duck breasts, skin side down, in the skillet to sear for about 2-3 minutes until the skin is golden brown.
- Flip the duck breasts and transfer the skillet to the preheated oven. Roast for about 10-15 minutes or until the duck is cooked to your liking.

- Let it rest for a few minutes before slicing it into thin strips.

For the Salad:

Prepare the Mango:
- Peel, pit, and dice the ripe mango.

Assemble the Salad:
- In a large bowl, combine diced mango, sliced red bell pepper, sliced cucumber, cherry tomatoes, sliced red onion, and chopped cilantro.

For the Dressing:

Prepare the Dressing:
- In a small bowl, whisk together olive oil, soy sauce, honey, lime juice, and sriracha until well combined.

Combine and Serve:
- Drizzle the dressing over the salad and toss until everything is well coated.
- Arrange the sliced duck on top of the salad.
- Garnish with additional cilantro if desired.

Optional: Serve with Noodles or Rice:
- For a heartier meal, you can serve the spicy mango duck salad over cooked noodles or rice.

Enjoy your Spicy Mango Duck Salad!

Honey-Glazed Duck Breast

Ingredients:

For the Duck:

- 2 duck breasts, skin-on
- Salt and black pepper, to taste

For the Honey Glaze:

- 1/4 cup honey
- 2 tablespoons soy sauce
- 1 tablespoon Dijon mustard
- 1 tablespoon balsamic vinegar
- 2 cloves garlic, minced
- 1 teaspoon fresh ginger, grated (optional)

Instructions:

Prepare the Duck:
- Pat the duck breasts dry with paper towels. Score the skin in a crosshatch pattern, being careful not to cut into the meat.
- Season both sides of the duck breasts with salt and black pepper.

Sear the Duck:
- Heat a skillet over medium-high heat. Place the duck breasts, skin side down, in the skillet. Sear for about 5-7 minutes or until the skin is golden brown and crispy.
- Flip the duck breasts and sear the other side for an additional 2-3 minutes.

Make the Honey Glaze:
- In a small bowl, whisk together honey, soy sauce, Dijon mustard, balsamic vinegar, minced garlic, and grated ginger (if using).

Glaze the Duck:
- Pour the honey glaze over the duck breasts. Use a brush to evenly coat the duck with the glaze.
- Let the duck cook for an additional 2-3 minutes, allowing the glaze to caramelize.

Rest and Slice:
- Remove the duck breasts from the skillet and let them rest for a few minutes on a cutting board.
- Slice the duck breast diagonally into thin slices.

Serve:
- Arrange the sliced duck on a serving plate. Drizzle any remaining honey glaze over the top.
- Optionally, serve the honey-glazed duck over a bed of sautéed vegetables, rice, or couscous.

Enjoy your Honey-Glazed Duck Breast!

Smoked Duck Breast with Raspberry Sauce

Ingredients:

For the Smoked Duck Breast:

- 2 duck breasts, skin-on
- Salt and black pepper, to taste
- 1 tablespoon olive oil
- Wood chips for smoking (applewood or cherry wood work well)

For the Raspberry Sauce:

- 1 cup fresh or frozen raspberries
- 2 tablespoons balsamic vinegar
- 2 tablespoons honey
- 1/4 cup red wine
- Salt and black pepper, to taste

Instructions:

For the Smoked Duck Breast:

> Prepare the Duck:
> - Pat the duck breasts dry with paper towels. Score the skin in a crosshatch pattern and season both sides with salt and black pepper.
>
> Brine (Optional):
> - For added flavor, you can brine the duck breasts in a solution of water, salt, and sugar for a few hours before smoking. Rinse and pat dry before proceeding.
>
> Preheat the Smoker:
> - Preheat your smoker to 225°F (107°C), adding the wood chips for smoking.
>
> Smoke the Duck:
> - Place the seasoned duck breasts directly on the smoker grate, skin side up.
> - Smoke the duck for about 1.5 to 2 hours or until the internal temperature reaches 165°F (74°C).
>
> Finish in the Oven (Optional):
> - If the skin is not as crispy as you'd like, you can finish the duck breasts in a preheated oven at 375°F (190°C) for 5-10 minutes.

For the Raspberry Sauce:

- Prepare the Sauce:
  - In a saucepan, combine raspberries, balsamic vinegar, honey, and red wine.
- Simmer:
  - Bring the mixture to a simmer over medium heat. Use a spoon to break down the raspberries and stir occasionally.
- Reduce and Season:
  - Let the sauce simmer until it thickens to your desired consistency. Season with salt and black pepper to taste.
- Strain (Optional):
  - If you prefer a smoother sauce, you can strain the raspberry sauce to remove the seeds.

Serve:

- Slice the smoked duck breasts diagonally into thin slices.
- Drizzle the raspberry sauce over the sliced duck or serve it on the side.
- Garnish with fresh raspberries and a sprig of mint, if desired.

Enjoy your Smoked Duck Breast with Raspberry Sauce!

Grilled Duck Skewers with Plum Sauce

Ingredients:

For the Duck Skewers:

- 2 duck breasts, skinless, boneless, cut into bite-sized pieces
- 1 tablespoon soy sauce
- 1 tablespoon hoisin sauce
- 1 tablespoon honey
- 1 tablespoon sesame oil
- 2 cloves garlic, minced
- 1 teaspoon fresh ginger, grated
- Wooden skewers, soaked in water for 30 minutes

For the Plum Sauce:

- 1 cup fresh or canned plums, pitted and chopped
- 2 tablespoons soy sauce
- 2 tablespoons rice vinegar
- 2 tablespoons honey
- 1 teaspoon sesame oil
- 1 teaspoon fresh ginger, grated
- 1 clove garlic, minced
- Red pepper flakes, to taste (optional for heat)

Instructions:

For the Duck Skewers:

    Prepare the Marinade:
- In a bowl, combine soy sauce, hoisin sauce, honey, sesame oil, minced garlic, and grated ginger.

    Marinate the Duck:
- Add the duck pieces to the marinade, ensuring they are well-coated. Let it marinate for at least 30 minutes or refrigerate for a few hours for better flavor.

    Skewer the Duck:
- Preheat the grill to medium-high heat.
- Thread the marinated duck pieces onto the soaked wooden skewers.

    Grill the Skewers:
- Grill the duck skewers for about 4-6 minutes per side or until the duck is cooked to your desired doneness and has a nice char.

For the Plum Sauce:

Prepare the Plum Sauce:
- In a saucepan, combine chopped plums, soy sauce, rice vinegar, honey, sesame oil, grated ginger, minced garlic, and red pepper flakes (if using).

Simmer:
- Bring the mixture to a simmer over medium heat. Cook for about 10-15 minutes until the plums break down and the sauce thickens.

Blend (Optional):
- For a smoother sauce, you can use an immersion blender or transfer the mixture to a blender and blend until smooth.

Adjust Seasoning:
- Taste the sauce and adjust the sweetness or spiciness according to your preference.

Serve:
- Arrange the grilled duck skewers on a serving platter.
- Drizzle the plum sauce over the skewers or serve it on the side for dipping.
- Garnish with chopped green onions or sesame seeds if desired.

Enjoy your Grilled Duck Skewers with Plum Sauce!

Duck Gumbo

Ingredients:

For the Duck:

- 2 duck leg quarters
- Salt and black pepper, to taste
- 1 teaspoon paprika
- 1 teaspoon dried thyme
- 1 teaspoon dried oregano
- 1/2 teaspoon cayenne pepper
- 1/4 cup all-purpose flour
- 2 tablespoons vegetable oil

For the Gumbo Base:

- 1/2 cup vegetable oil
- 1/2 cup all-purpose flour
- 1 large onion, diced
- 1 bell pepper, diced
- 2 celery stalks, diced
- 3 cloves garlic, minced
- 1 pound andouille sausage, sliced
- 4 cups chicken or duck broth
- 1 can (14 oz) crushed tomatoes
- 1 bay leaf
- 1 teaspoon dried thyme
- 1 teaspoon dried oregano
- Salt and black pepper, to taste
- Cooked white rice, for serving
- Chopped green onions and fresh parsley, for garnish

Instructions:

For the Duck:

Season the Duck:
- In a bowl, combine salt, black pepper, paprika, dried thyme, dried oregano, cayenne pepper, and flour.
- Season the duck leg quarters with the spice mixture, ensuring they are well coated.

Brown the Duck:
- Heat 2 tablespoons of vegetable oil in a large, heavy pot or Dutch oven over medium-high heat.
- Brown the duck leg quarters on both sides. Remove and set aside.

For the Gumbo Base:

Prepare the Roux:
- In the same pot, add 1/2 cup of vegetable oil. Gradually whisk in 1/2 cup of flour to create a roux.
- Cook the roux over medium heat, stirring constantly, until it reaches a dark brown color. Be careful not to burn it.

Sauté Vegetables:
- Add diced onion, bell pepper, celery, and minced garlic to the roux. Sauté until the vegetables are softened.

Add Sausage:
- Stir in the sliced andouille sausage and cook for a few minutes until it starts to brown.

Combine Broth and Tomatoes:
- Gradually add the chicken or duck broth while stirring to avoid lumps.
- Add crushed tomatoes, bay leaf, dried thyme, dried oregano, salt, and black pepper. Bring the mixture to a simmer.

Simmer with Duck:
- Return the browned duck leg quarters to the pot. Cover and simmer over low heat for about 2 hours until the duck is tender and the flavors meld.

Serve:
- Remove the bay leaf and discard. Serve the gumbo over cooked white rice.
- Garnish with chopped green onions and fresh parsley.

Enjoy your hearty Duck Gumbo!

Duck and Black Bean Enchiladas

Ingredients:

For the Duck Filling:

- 2 duck breasts, cooked and shredded
- 1 tablespoon olive oil
- 1 small onion, finely chopped
- 2 cloves garlic, minced
- 1 teaspoon ground cumin
- 1 teaspoon chili powder
- Salt and black pepper, to taste
- 1 can (15 oz) black beans, drained and rinsed
- 1 cup corn kernels (fresh or frozen)
- 1 cup shredded Monterey Jack or Mexican blend cheese
- 1/4 cup fresh cilantro, chopped

For the Enchilada Sauce:

- 2 tablespoons olive oil
- 2 tablespoons all-purpose flour
- 2 tablespoons chili powder
- 1 teaspoon ground cumin
- 1/2 teaspoon garlic powder
- 1/2 teaspoon onion powder
- 1/4 teaspoon cayenne pepper (optional, for heat)
- 1 can (14 oz) crushed tomatoes
- 1 cup chicken or vegetable broth
- Salt and black pepper, to taste

For Assembling:

- 8-10 flour tortillas
- 1 cup shredded cheese for topping (Monterey Jack or Mexican blend)
- Fresh cilantro and sliced green onions for garnish
- Sour cream and sliced jalapeños (optional, for serving)

Instructions:

For the Duck Filling:

Cook and Shred Duck:
- Cook the duck breasts until fully cooked. Shred the meat using forks or your fingers.

Sauté Duck and Vegetables:
- In a skillet, heat olive oil over medium heat. Sauté the chopped onion until translucent.
- Add minced garlic, shredded duck, ground cumin, chili powder, salt, and black pepper. Cook for a few minutes until well combined.
- Stir in black beans, corn, shredded cheese, and fresh cilantro. Cook until the cheese is melted and the mixture is heated through.

For the Enchilada Sauce:

Prepare the Sauce:
- In a saucepan, heat olive oil over medium heat. Whisk in the flour, chili powder, ground cumin, garlic powder, onion powder, and cayenne pepper (if using).
- Gradually whisk in crushed tomatoes and chicken or vegetable broth. Simmer for 10-15 minutes until the sauce thickens.
- Season with salt and black pepper to taste.

Assembling the Enchiladas:

Preheat Oven:
- Preheat your oven to 375°F (190°C).

Prepare a Baking Dish:
- Spread a small amount of the enchilada sauce on the bottom of a baking dish.

Fill and Roll:
- Place a generous amount of the duck and black bean mixture onto each flour tortilla.
- Roll up the tortillas and place them seam side down in the baking dish.

Cover with Sauce:
- Pour the remaining enchilada sauce over the rolled tortillas.
- Sprinkle shredded cheese over the top.

Bake:
- Bake in the preheated oven for about 20-25 minutes or until the cheese is melted and bubbly.

Serve:
- Garnish with fresh cilantro and sliced green onions.
- Optionally, serve with sour cream and sliced jalapeños on the side.

Enjoy your Duck and Black Bean Enchiladas!

Duck and Cherry Sauce

Ingredients:

For the Duck:

- 2 duck breasts, skin-on
- Salt and black pepper, to taste
- 1 tablespoon olive oil

For the Cherry Sauce:

- 1 cup fresh or frozen cherries, pitted and halved
- 1/4 cup red wine
- 2 tablespoons balsamic vinegar
- 2 tablespoons honey
- 1 tablespoon soy sauce
- 1 teaspoon cornstarch (optional, for thickening)
- Salt and black pepper, to taste

For Garnish:

- Fresh parsley, chopped

Instructions:

For the Duck:

Score and Season the Duck:
- Score the duck skin in a crisscross pattern, being careful not to cut into the meat.
- Season both sides of the duck breasts with salt and black pepper.

Sear the Duck:
- Heat olive oil in a skillet over medium-high heat.
- Place the duck breasts in the skillet, skin side down, and sear for about 5-7 minutes until the skin is golden and crispy.
- Flip and sear the other side for an additional 2-3 minutes.
- Adjust heat if necessary to render the fat from the skin.

Finish Cooking:
- Reduce heat to medium and continue cooking for another 5-7 minutes or until the internal temperature reaches your desired doneness (medium-rare to medium).
- Let the duck rest for a few minutes before slicing.

For the Cherry Sauce:

- Prepare the Sauce:
    - In the same skillet, combine cherries, red wine, balsamic vinegar, honey, and soy sauce.
    - Bring the mixture to a simmer over medium heat.
- Thicken the Sauce (Optional):
    - If you prefer a thicker sauce, mix cornstarch with a little water to create a slurry. Stir the slurry into the cherry mixture and cook for an additional 2-3 minutes until thickened.
- Season the Sauce:
    - Season the cherry sauce with salt and black pepper to taste.

Serve:

- Slice the duck breasts diagonally into thin slices.
- Arrange the duck slices on a plate and drizzle the cherry sauce over the top.
- Garnish with fresh chopped parsley.

Enjoy your Duck with Cherry Sauce! This dish pairs well with a side of roasted vegetables or mashed potatoes.

Duck Spring Rolls

Ingredients:

For the Duck:

- 2 duck breasts, skin-on
- Salt and black pepper, to taste
- 1 tablespoon hoisin sauce
- 1 tablespoon soy sauce
- 1 tablespoon sesame oil

For the Spring Rolls:

- Rice paper wrappers
- Rice vermicelli noodles, cooked according to package instructions
- Shredded lettuce
- Shredded carrots
- Bean sprouts
- Fresh mint leaves
- Fresh cilantro leaves
- Spring onions, thinly sliced

For the Dipping Sauce:

- 1/4 cup hoisin sauce
- 2 tablespoons soy sauce
- 1 tablespoon rice vinegar
- 1 teaspoon sesame oil
- Crushed peanuts for garnish (optional)

Instructions:

For the Duck:

> Prepare the Duck:
> - Preheat your oven to 400°F (200°C).
> - Score the duck skin in a crisscross pattern, being careful not to cut into the meat.
> - Season the duck breasts with salt and black pepper.
> - In a small bowl, mix hoisin sauce, soy sauce, and sesame oil.
> - Brush the duck breasts with the hoisin mixture.
>
> Roast the Duck:

- Place the duck breasts on a baking sheet and roast in the preheated oven for about 15-20 minutes or until the skin is crispy and the duck is cooked to your liking.
- Let the duck rest for a few minutes, then slice it into thin strips.

For the Spring Rolls:

Prepare the Rice Paper Wrappers:
- Fill a shallow dish with warm water. Dip each rice paper wrapper into the water for about 5-10 seconds until it softens. Place it on a clean, damp kitchen towel.

Assemble the Spring Rolls:
- In the center of the rice paper wrapper, place a small portion of cooked rice vermicelli noodles.
- Add shredded lettuce, shredded carrots, bean sprouts, fresh mint leaves, cilantro leaves, spring onions, and slices of the roasted duck.

Roll the Spring Rolls:
- Fold the sides of the rice paper over the filling and then roll tightly from the bottom to the top.

Repeat:
- Repeat the process with the remaining ingredients.

For the Dipping Sauce:

Prepare the Sauce:
- In a small bowl, whisk together hoisin sauce, soy sauce, rice vinegar, and sesame oil.

Serve:
- Serve the Duck Spring Rolls with the dipping sauce.
- Optionally, garnish the dipping sauce with crushed peanuts.

Enjoy your Duck Spring Rolls as a delightful appetizer or light meal!

Teriyaki Duck Noodles

Ingredients:

For the Teriyaki Duck:

- 2 duck breasts, skin-on
- Salt and black pepper, to taste
- 1/4 cup soy sauce
- 2 tablespoons mirin
- 2 tablespoons sake or rice wine
- 2 tablespoons honey
- 1 tablespoon sesame oil
- 2 cloves garlic, minced
- 1 teaspoon fresh ginger, grated

For the Noodles:

- 8 oz (about 225g) egg noodles or udon noodles
- 1 tablespoon vegetable oil
- 1 red bell pepper, thinly sliced
- 1 carrot, julienned
- 1 cup broccoli florets
- 2 green onions, sliced
- Sesame seeds for garnish

Instructions:

For the Teriyaki Duck:

    Prepare the Duck:
- Score the duck skin in a crisscross pattern. Season both sides with salt and black pepper.

    Make the Teriyaki Sauce:
- In a bowl, mix together soy sauce, mirin, sake or rice wine, honey, sesame oil, minced garlic, and grated ginger.

    Marinate the Duck:
- Place the duck breasts in a shallow dish and pour half of the teriyaki sauce over them. Let it marinate for at least 30 minutes.

    Cook the Duck:
- Preheat your oven to 400°F (200°C).

- Heat a skillet over medium-high heat. Sear the duck breasts, skin side down, for 2-3 minutes until the skin is golden.
- Flip the duck breasts and transfer the skillet to the preheated oven. Roast for about 10-15 minutes or until the duck is cooked to your liking.
- While roasting, baste the duck with the remaining teriyaki sauce a couple of times.
- Let the duck rest for a few minutes before slicing it into thin strips.

For the Noodles:

Cook the Noodles:
- Cook the egg noodles or udon noodles according to the package instructions. Drain and set aside.

Stir-Fry Vegetables:
- In a large skillet or wok, heat vegetable oil over medium-high heat.
- Add sliced red bell pepper, julienned carrot, and broccoli florets. Stir-fry for 3-4 minutes until the vegetables are tender-crisp.

Combine Noodles and Vegetables:
- Add the cooked noodles to the skillet with the stir-fried vegetables. Toss to combine.

Assemble:
- Serve the teriyaki duck slices on top of the noodles and vegetables.
- Garnish with sliced green onions and sesame seeds.

Enjoy your Teriyaki Duck Noodles! This dish combines the rich flavors of teriyaki duck with the savory goodness of stir-fried noodles and vegetables.

Duck and Cranberry Stuffed Acorn Squash

Ingredients:

For the Stuffed Acorn Squash:

- 2 acorn squash, halved and seeds removed
- 2 duck breasts, skin-on
- Salt and black pepper, to taste
- 2 tablespoons olive oil
- 1 cup wild rice, cooked according to package instructions
- 1/2 cup dried cranberries
- 1/2 cup pecans, chopped
- 1/4 cup fresh parsley, chopped

For the Maple Glaze:

- 1/4 cup maple syrup
- 2 tablespoons balsamic vinegar
- 1 tablespoon Dijon mustard
- 1 clove garlic, minced
- Salt and black pepper, to taste

Instructions:

For the Stuffed Acorn Squash:

Preheat Oven:
- Preheat your oven to 400°F (200°C).

Prepare Acorn Squash:
- Cut the acorn squash in half, scoop out the seeds, and place the halves on a baking sheet.
- Drizzle olive oil over the squash halves and season with salt and black pepper.
- Roast in the preheated oven for about 30-40 minutes or until the squash is fork-tender.

Cook the Duck:
- While the squash is roasting, season the duck breasts with salt and black pepper.
- In a skillet over medium-high heat, sear the duck breasts, skin side down, for about 5-7 minutes until the skin is crispy.

- Flip the duck breasts and cook for an additional 4-5 minutes or until cooked to your liking.
- Let the duck rest for a few minutes before slicing it into thin strips.

Prepare the Filling:
- In a bowl, mix the cooked wild rice, dried cranberries, chopped pecans, and fresh parsley.
- Add the sliced duck breasts to the mixture.

Stuff the Squash:
- Once the acorn squash halves are cooked, fill each half with the duck and wild rice mixture.

For the Maple Glaze:

Prepare the Glaze:
- In a small saucepan, combine maple syrup, balsamic vinegar, Dijon mustard, minced garlic, salt, and black pepper.
- Cook over medium heat, stirring, until the glaze is heated through and slightly thickened.

Drizzle the Glaze:
- Drizzle the maple glaze over the stuffed acorn squash.

Serve:
- Garnish with additional fresh parsley.
- Serve the Duck and Cranberry Stuffed Acorn Squash warm.

Enjoy this delightful and festive dish with the combination of savory duck, sweet cranberries, and the richness of the acorn squash!

Thai Red Curry Duck

Ingredients:

For the Duck:

- 2 duck breasts, skin-on
- Salt and black pepper, to taste
- 1 tablespoon vegetable oil

For the Red Curry Sauce:

- 2 tablespoons red curry paste
- 1 can (14 oz) coconut milk
- 1 tablespoon fish sauce
- 1 tablespoon soy sauce
- 1 tablespoon brown sugar
- 1 red bell pepper, sliced
- 1 yellow bell pepper, sliced
- 1 zucchini, sliced
- 1 cup cherry tomatoes, halved
- 1 cup baby spinach leaves
- Fresh cilantro, for garnish
- Cooked jasmine rice, for serving

Instructions:

For the Duck:

　Prepare the Duck:
- Score the duck skin in a crisscross pattern, being careful not to cut into the meat.
- Season both sides of the duck breasts with salt and black pepper.

　Sear the Duck:
- Heat vegetable oil in a skillet over medium-high heat.
- Place the duck breasts in the skillet, skin side down, and sear for about 5-7 minutes until the skin is golden and crispy.
- Flip the duck breasts and sear the other side for an additional 2-3 minutes.
- Transfer the duck to a cutting board and let it rest for a few minutes before slicing it into thin strips.

For the Red Curry Sauce:

> Prepare the Sauce:
> - In the same skillet, add red curry paste and cook over medium heat for 1-2 minutes until fragrant.
>
> Add Coconut Milk:
> - Pour in the coconut milk and stir to combine with the curry paste.
>
> Season the Sauce:
> - Add fish sauce, soy sauce, and brown sugar. Stir well to combine.
>
> Add Vegetables:
> - Add sliced red bell pepper, yellow bell pepper, zucchini, and cherry tomatoes to the sauce. Simmer for 5-7 minutes until the vegetables are tender.
>
> Add Spinach:
> - Add baby spinach leaves to the curry and cook until wilted.
>
> Combine with Duck:
> - Gently stir in the sliced duck to the curry mixture. Allow it to heat through for a few minutes.

Serve:

- Serve the Thai Red Curry Duck over cooked jasmine rice.
- Garnish with fresh cilantro.

Enjoy your Thai Red Curry Duck, a flavorful and aromatic dish with the perfect balance of spice and creaminess!

Citrus-Marinated Grilled Duck

Ingredients:

For the Marinade:

- 2 duck breasts, skin-on
- Zest and juice of 1 orange
- Zest and juice of 1 lemon
- Zest and juice of 1 lime
- 3 tablespoons olive oil
- 2 cloves garlic, minced
- 1 tablespoon honey
- 1 teaspoon Dijon mustard
- Salt and black pepper, to taste

For the Garnish:

- Fresh herbs (such as parsley or cilantro), chopped
- Citrus slices for garnish

Instructions:

For the Marinade:

   Prepare the Marinade:
   - In a bowl, whisk together the orange zest, orange juice, lemon zest, lemon juice, lime zest, lime juice, olive oil, minced garlic, honey, Dijon mustard, salt, and black pepper.

   Marinate the Duck:
   - Place the duck breasts in a shallow dish or a resealable plastic bag.
   - Pour the marinade over the duck, ensuring that it is well-coated.
   - Marinate in the refrigerator for at least 2 hours, or preferably overnight for enhanced flavor.

Grilling the Duck:

   Preheat the Grill:
   - Preheat your grill to medium-high heat.

   Remove Duck from Marinade:

- Remove the duck breasts from the marinade and let them come to room temperature.

Grill the Duck:
- Place the duck breasts on the preheated grill, skin side down.
- Grill for about 5-7 minutes per side, or until the skin is crispy and the internal temperature reaches your desired level of doneness.

Baste with Marinade:
- During the grilling process, baste the duck with the remaining marinade to keep it moist and add extra flavor.

Rest and Slice:
- Once cooked, let the duck rest for a few minutes before slicing it into thin strips.

Serve:

- Arrange the sliced citrus-marinated grilled duck on a serving platter.
- Garnish with chopped fresh herbs and citrus slices.

Enjoy your Citrus-Marinated Grilled Duck with its bright and zesty flavors! This dish pairs well with a side of roasted vegetables or a fresh salad.

Duck and Fig Pizza

Ingredients:

For the Pizza:

- 1 pizza dough (store-bought or homemade)
- 1 cup cooked and shredded duck meat (from duck breasts)
- 1/2 cup fig jam
- 1 cup fresh figs, sliced
- 1 cup mozzarella cheese, shredded
- 1/2 cup blue cheese, crumbled
- Fresh arugula, for topping
- Balsamic glaze, for drizzling

Optional Toppings:

- Caramelized onions
- Prosciutto slices
- Fresh thyme leaves

Instructions:

    Preheat the Oven:
- Preheat your oven according to the pizza dough package instructions or your homemade pizza dough recipe.

    Roll Out the Dough:
- Roll out the pizza dough on a floured surface to your desired thickness.

    Assemble the Pizza:
- Spread fig jam evenly over the pizza dough, leaving a small border around the edges.
- Distribute the shredded duck meat over the jam.
- Sprinkle mozzarella cheese over the duck and jam.
- Place fresh fig slices evenly on top, followed by crumbled blue cheese.

    Bake the Pizza:
- Transfer the assembled pizza to a preheated pizza stone or a baking sheet.
- Bake according to the dough instructions or until the crust is golden and the cheese is melted and bubbly.

    Add Fresh Toppings:

- Once out of the oven, add fresh arugula on top of the hot pizza. The heat will slightly wilt the arugula.

Optional Toppings:
- Add optional toppings like caramelized onions, prosciutto slices, or fresh thyme leaves.

Drizzle with Balsamic Glaze:
- Drizzle balsamic glaze over the finished pizza for an extra burst of flavor.

Slice and Serve:
- Allow the pizza to cool for a few minutes before slicing.
- Serve slices of the Duck and Fig Pizza and enjoy!

This unique pizza combines the richness of duck with the sweetness of figs, creating a delightful blend of flavors. Customize it with your favorite toppings for a personalized touch.

Hoisin-Glazed Duck Wings

Ingredients:

For the Duck Wings:

- 2 lbs duck wings, split at joints
- Salt and black pepper, to taste
- 1 tablespoon vegetable oil

For the Hoisin Glaze:

- 1/4 cup hoisin sauce
- 2 tablespoons soy sauce
- 2 tablespoons honey
- 1 tablespoon rice vinegar
- 1 tablespoon sesame oil
- 2 cloves garlic, minced
- 1 teaspoon fresh ginger, grated
- 1 tablespoon chopped green onions (for garnish, optional)
- Sesame seeds (for garnish, optional)

Instructions:

For the Duck Wings:

- Preheat the Oven:
  - Preheat your oven to 400°F (200°C).
- Season the Wings:
  - Pat the duck wings dry with paper towels. Season with salt and black pepper.
- Bake the Wings:
  - Place the wings on a baking sheet lined with parchment paper.
  - Bake in the preheated oven for about 40-45 minutes or until the wings are golden and crispy.
- Prepare the Hoisin Glaze:
  - While the wings are baking, prepare the hoisin glaze. In a bowl, whisk together hoisin sauce, soy sauce, honey, rice vinegar, sesame oil, minced garlic, and grated ginger.
- Glaze the Wings:
  - In the last 10 minutes of baking, brush the duck wings with a generous coating of the hoisin glaze.
- Broil (Optional):

- If you want a charred finish, you can broil the wings for an additional 2-3 minutes after glazing, but keep a close eye to prevent burning.

Garnish:
- Once out of the oven, sprinkle chopped green onions and sesame seeds over the glazed wings for garnish.

Serve:
- Serve the Hoisin-Glazed Duck Wings warm.
- Optionally, serve with extra hoisin sauce for dipping.

Enjoy these flavorful and sticky Hoisin-Glazed Duck Wings as a delightful appetizer or party snack!

Mediterranean Duck Salad

Ingredients:

For the Duck:

- 2 duck breasts, skin-on
- Salt and black pepper, to taste
- 1 tablespoon olive oil

For the Salad:

- Mixed salad greens (e.g., arugula, spinach, watercress)
- Cherry tomatoes, halved
- Cucumber, sliced
- Kalamata olives, pitted
- Red onion, thinly sliced
- Feta cheese, crumbled

For the Dressing:

- 3 tablespoons extra-virgin olive oil
- 1 tablespoon balsamic vinegar
- 1 teaspoon Dijon mustard
- 1 clove garlic, minced
- Salt and black pepper, to taste
- Fresh oregano or basil, chopped (optional, for garnish)

Instructions:

For the Duck:

  Prepare the Duck:
  - Score the duck skin in a crisscross pattern. Season both sides of the duck breasts with salt and black pepper.

  Sear the Duck:
  - Heat olive oil in a skillet over medium-high heat.
  - Place the duck breasts in the skillet, skin side down, and sear for about 5-7 minutes until the skin is golden and crispy.
  - Flip the duck breasts and sear the other side for an additional 2-3 minutes.

- Transfer the duck to a cutting board and let it rest for a few minutes before slicing it into thin strips.

For the Salad:

Assemble the Salad:
- In a large salad bowl, combine the mixed salad greens, cherry tomatoes, cucumber slices, Kalamata olives, red onion, and crumbled feta cheese.

Add the Sliced Duck:
- Arrange the sliced duck on top of the salad.

For the Dressing:

Prepare the Dressing:
- In a small bowl, whisk together extra-virgin olive oil, balsamic vinegar, Dijon mustard, minced garlic, salt, and black pepper.

Dress the Salad:
- Drizzle the dressing over the salad and gently toss to coat.

Garnish:
- Garnish with fresh oregano or basil if desired.

Serve:
- Serve the Mediterranean Duck Salad immediately.

Enjoy this Mediterranean-inspired Duck Salad as a light and flavorful meal with the perfect balance of savory duck, crisp vegetables, and tangy dressing!

Duck Liver Pâté

Ingredients:

- 1 pound duck livers, trimmed
- 1 cup finely chopped shallots
- 2 cloves garlic, minced
- 1/2 cup unsalted butter
- 1/4 cup brandy or cognac
- 1 teaspoon dried thyme
- 1 teaspoon dried rosemary
- Salt and black pepper, to taste
- 1/2 cup heavy cream
- 2 tablespoons clarified butter (for sealing)

Instructions:

Clean and Trim Duck Livers:
- Rinse the duck livers under cold water and pat them dry with paper towels. Trim any connective tissues or membranes.

Sauté Shallots and Garlic:
- In a skillet over medium heat, melt 2 tablespoons of butter. Add finely chopped shallots and minced garlic. Sauté until softened.

Cook Livers:
- Add duck livers to the skillet. Cook for about 5-7 minutes until they are browned on the outside but slightly pink in the center. Overcooking can result in a grainy texture.

Deglaze with Brandy:
- Pour brandy or cognac into the skillet to deglaze, scraping up any browned bits from the bottom of the pan. Allow the alcohol to evaporate.

Add Herbs and Seasonings:
- Sprinkle dried thyme, dried rosemary, salt, and black pepper over the livers. Stir to combine.

Blend in Food Processor:
- Transfer the cooked livers and shallot mixture to a food processor. Process until smooth.

Add Heavy Cream:
- With the food processor running, gradually pour in the heavy cream. Continue processing until the mixture is silky and well combined.

Adjust Seasoning:

- Taste the pâté and adjust the seasoning if needed.

Strain (Optional):
- For an extra-smooth texture, you can strain the pâté through a fine mesh sieve or cheesecloth to remove any remaining solids.

Pack into Jars:
- Spoon the pâté into jars or ramekins, leveling the surface.

Seal with Clarified Butter:
- Melt the clarified butter and pour a thin layer over the top of each jar. This helps to seal and preserve the pâté.

Chill:
- Refrigerate the duck liver pâté for at least a few hours or overnight to allow the flavors to meld and the texture to set.

Serve:
- Serve the pâté with crusty bread, crackers, or sliced baguette.

Enjoy your homemade Duck Liver Pâté as an elegant appetizer or spread for special occasions!

Moroccan Spiced Duck Tagine

Ingredients:

For the Duck:

- 2 duck legs or duck breasts, skin-on
- Salt and black pepper, to taste
- 2 tablespoons olive oil

For the Tagine:

- 1 large onion, finely chopped
- 3 cloves garlic, minced
- 1 teaspoon ground cumin
- 1 teaspoon ground coriander
- 1 teaspoon ground cinnamon
- 1 teaspoon paprika
- 1/2 teaspoon ground ginger
- 1/2 teaspoon ground turmeric
- 1/4 teaspoon cayenne pepper (adjust to taste)
- 1 can (14 oz) diced tomatoes, undrained
- 1 cup chicken or vegetable broth
- 1 cup dried apricots, halved
- 1/2 cup green olives, pitted
- Zest and juice of 1 orange
- Fresh cilantro or parsley, chopped (for garnish)
- Cooked couscous or rice (for serving)

Instructions:

For the Duck:

    Preheat the Oven:
- Preheat your oven to 325°F (163°C).

    Season the Duck:
- Pat the duck legs or breasts dry with paper towels. Season with salt and black pepper.

    Sear the Duck:
- Heat olive oil in a large, ovenproof skillet or tagine over medium-high heat. Sear the duck on all sides until browned. Remove the duck from the skillet and set aside.

For the Tagine:

- Sauté Aromatics:
  - In the same skillet or tagine, add chopped onion and garlic. Sauté until softened.
- Add Spices:
  - Add ground cumin, ground coriander, ground cinnamon, paprika, ground ginger, ground turmeric, and cayenne pepper. Stir to coat the onions and garlic with the spices.
- Combine Tomatoes and Broth:
  - Pour in the diced tomatoes with their juices and chicken or vegetable broth. Stir well to combine.
- Return Duck to the Tagine:
  - Place the seared duck legs or breasts back into the skillet or tagine, nestling them into the sauce.
- Add Apricots and Olives:
  - Scatter halved dried apricots and green olives around the duck.
- Zest and Juice:
  - Zest and juice the orange, adding both to the tagine.
- Bake:
  - Cover the skillet or tagine and transfer it to the preheated oven. Bake for about 1.5 to 2 hours or until the duck is tender and the flavors meld.
- Adjust Seasoning:
  - Taste the tagine and adjust seasoning if needed.
- Serve:
  - Serve the Moroccan Spiced Duck Tagine over cooked couscous or rice.
- Garnish:
  - Garnish with chopped fresh cilantro or parsley.

Enjoy this Moroccan-inspired dish with tender duck, aromatic spices, and the sweetness of apricots!

Duck and Blueberry Balsamic Reduction

Ingredients:

For the Duck:

- 2 duck breasts, skin-on
- Salt and black pepper, to taste
- 1 tablespoon olive oil

For the Blueberry Balsamic Reduction:

- 1 cup fresh or frozen blueberries
- 1/2 cup balsamic vinegar
- 2 tablespoons honey
- 1 teaspoon Dijon mustard
- Salt and black pepper, to taste

For Garnish:

- Fresh thyme leaves
- Blueberries

Instructions:

For the Duck:

    Prepare the Duck:
- Score the duck skin in a crisscross pattern. Season both sides of the duck breasts with salt and black pepper.

    Sear the Duck:
- Heat olive oil in a skillet over medium-high heat.
- Place the duck breasts in the skillet, skin side down, and sear for about 5-7 minutes until the skin is golden and crispy.
- Flip the duck breasts and sear the other side for an additional 2-3 minutes.
- Transfer the duck to a cutting board and let it rest for a few minutes before slicing it into thin strips.

For the Blueberry Balsamic Reduction:

    Prepare the Reduction:
- In a small saucepan, combine blueberries, balsamic vinegar, honey, Dijon mustard, salt, and black pepper.

Simmer:
- Bring the mixture to a simmer over medium heat.

Cook Down:
- Reduce the heat to low and let it simmer for about 10-15 minutes, or until the blueberries have burst and the sauce has thickened.

Strain (Optional):
- If you prefer a smoother sauce, you can strain the reduction to remove the blueberry solids.

Serve:

- Arrange the sliced duck on a serving plate.
- Drizzle the Blueberry Balsamic Reduction over the duck.
- Garnish with fresh thyme leaves and additional blueberries.

Enjoy your Duck with Blueberry Balsamic Reduction, a delightful combination of savory duck with the sweet and tangy flavors of the blueberry balsamic sauce! Serve it with your favorite side dishes for a complete and flavorful meal.

Duck Sausage and Apple-Stuffed Squash

Ingredients:

For the Stuffed Squash:

- 2 acorn squash, halved and seeds removed
- 1 tablespoon olive oil
- Salt and black pepper, to taste

For the Filling:

- 1 lb duck sausage, casings removed
- 1 tablespoon olive oil
- 1 onion, finely chopped
- 2 cloves garlic, minced
- 2 apples, peeled, cored, and diced
- 1/2 cup dried cranberries
- 1/2 cup chopped pecans
- 1 teaspoon fresh sage, chopped
- Salt and black pepper, to taste

For the Maple Glaze:

- 1/4 cup maple syrup
- 2 tablespoons balsamic vinegar
- 1 tablespoon Dijon mustard
- Salt and black pepper, to taste

Instructions:

For the Stuffed Squash:

    Preheat the Oven:
- Preheat your oven to 375°F (190°C).

    Prepare the Squash:
- Brush the cut sides of the acorn squash with olive oil and season with salt and black pepper.
- Place the squash halves, cut side down, on a baking sheet.

    Roast the Squash:

- Roast in the preheated oven for about 30-40 minutes or until the squash is tender when pierced with a fork.

For the Filling:

Cook the Duck Sausage:
- In a skillet over medium heat, cook the duck sausage, breaking it apart with a spoon until browned and cooked through. Remove from the skillet and set aside.

Sauté Onion and Garlic:
- In the same skillet, add olive oil. Sauté the chopped onion until softened, then add minced garlic and cook for an additional minute.

Add Apples and Cranberries:
- Stir in diced apples and dried cranberries. Cook for 3-5 minutes until the apples are slightly softened.

Combine Ingredients:
- Add the cooked duck sausage back to the skillet.
- Mix in chopped pecans and fresh sage.
- Season with salt and black pepper to taste. Stir to combine.

Assemble and Finish:

Stuff the Squash:
- Flip the roasted squash halves, cut side up.
- Fill each squash half with the duck sausage and apple mixture.

Prepare the Maple Glaze:
- In a small saucepan, combine maple syrup, balsamic vinegar, Dijon mustard, salt, and black pepper. Heat over low heat until warmed through.

Glaze and Bake:
- Brush the stuffed squash with the maple glaze.
- Return to the oven and bake for an additional 15-20 minutes or until the filling is heated through and the tops are slightly caramelized.

Serve:
- Drizzle with additional maple glaze before serving.
- Enjoy your Duck Sausage and Apple-Stuffed Squash!

This dish brings together the richness of duck sausage, the sweetness of apples, and the earthy flavors of acorn squash for a comforting and satisfying meal.

Duck and Port Wine Reduction

Ingredients:

For the Duck:

- 2 duck breasts, skin-on
- Salt and black pepper, to taste
- 1 tablespoon olive oil

For the Port Wine Reduction:

- 1 cup port wine
- 1/2 cup chicken or beef broth
- 2 tablespoons unsalted butter
- 1 tablespoon shallots, finely chopped
- 1 tablespoon honey
- Salt and black pepper, to taste

For Garnish:

- Fresh thyme leaves
- Pomegranate arils (optional)

Instructions:

For the Duck:

   Prepare the Duck:
   - Score the duck skin in a crisscross pattern. Season both sides of the duck breasts with salt and black pepper.

   Sear the Duck:
   - Heat olive oil in a skillet over medium-high heat.
   - Place the duck breasts in the skillet, skin side down, and sear for about 5-7 minutes until the skin is golden and crispy.
   - Flip the duck breasts and sear the other side for an additional 2-3 minutes.
   - Transfer the duck to a cutting board and let it rest for a few minutes before slicing it into thin strips.

For the Port Wine Reduction:

   Sauté Shallots:
   - In the same skillet, add chopped shallots and sauté until softened.

Deglaze with Port Wine:
- Pour in the port wine to deglaze the pan, scraping up any browned bits from the bottom.

Add Broth and Honey:
- Add chicken or beef broth and honey to the skillet. Stir well to combine.

Simmer:
- Allow the mixture to simmer over medium heat until it reduces by half.

Finish with Butter:
- Reduce the heat to low and whisk in unsalted butter until the sauce is smooth and glossy.

Season:
- Season the port wine reduction with salt and black pepper to taste.

Serve:
- Arrange the sliced duck on a serving plate.
- Drizzle the Port Wine Reduction over the duck.
- Garnish with fresh thyme leaves and pomegranate arils if desired.

Enjoy your Duck with Port Wine Reduction! This dish offers a perfect balance of rich duck flavors complemented by the sweet and savory notes of the port wine reduction. Serve it with your favorite side dishes for an elegant meal.

Spicy Cajun Duck Pasta

Ingredients:

For the Cajun Duck:

- 2 duck breasts, skin-on
- 2 tablespoons Cajun seasoning
- Salt and black pepper, to taste
- 2 tablespoons olive oil

For the Pasta:

- 8 oz (about 225g) fettuccine or your favorite pasta
- 1 tablespoon olive oil
- 1 onion, finely chopped
- 3 cloves garlic, minced
- 1 bell pepper, thinly sliced
- 1 cup cherry tomatoes, halved
- 1 cup heavy cream
- 1 teaspoon Cajun seasoning (adjust to taste)
- Salt and black pepper, to taste
- Fresh parsley, chopped (for garnish)
- Grated Parmesan cheese (for serving)

Instructions:

For the Cajun Duck:

Prepare the Duck:
- Score the duck skin in a crisscross pattern. Season both sides of the duck breasts with Cajun seasoning, salt, and black pepper.

Sear the Duck:
- Heat olive oil in a skillet over medium-high heat.
- Place the duck breasts in the skillet, skin side down, and sear for about 5-7 minutes until the skin is golden and crispy.
- Flip the duck breasts and sear the other side for an additional 2-3 minutes.
- Transfer the duck to a cutting board and let it rest for a few minutes before slicing it into thin strips.

For the Pasta:

Cook the Pasta:
- Cook the fettuccine or pasta according to the package instructions. Drain and set aside.

Sauté Vegetables:
- In a large skillet, heat olive oil over medium heat. Add chopped onion, minced garlic, and sliced bell pepper. Sauté until the vegetables are softened.

Add Tomatoes and Cream:
- Add halved cherry tomatoes to the skillet. Pour in the heavy cream and stir to combine.

Season:
- Season the sauce with Cajun seasoning, salt, and black pepper. Adjust the seasoning according to your taste.

Combine with Pasta:
- Add the cooked and drained pasta to the skillet. Toss everything together until the pasta is coated in the creamy Cajun sauce.

Serve:
- Plate the Cajun Duck Pasta and top it with sliced Cajun duck.
- Garnish with chopped fresh parsley and grated Parmesan cheese.

Enjoy your Spicy Cajun Duck Pasta, a delightful combination of succulent duck, bold Cajun flavors, and creamy pasta!

Duck Ravioli with Sage Brown Butter

Ingredients:

For the Duck Filling:

- 1 cup cooked and shredded duck meat (from duck legs or breasts)
- 1/2 cup ricotta cheese
- 1/4 cup grated Parmesan cheese
- 1 egg
- Salt and black pepper, to taste
- Fresh parsley, chopped (for garnish)

For the Pasta Dough (or use store-bought):

- 2 cups all-purpose flour
- 3 large eggs
- 1/2 teaspoon salt

For the Sage Brown Butter Sauce:

- 1/2 cup unsalted butter
- Fresh sage leaves
- Salt, to taste
- Grated Parmesan cheese (for serving)

Instructions:

For the Duck Filling:

Prepare the Duck:
- Cook duck legs or breasts until fully cooked. Shred the meat.

Make the Filling:
- In a bowl, combine the shredded duck meat, ricotta cheese, grated Parmesan cheese, egg, salt, and black pepper. Mix well until the filling is evenly combined.

For the Pasta Dough:

Make the Pasta Dough:
- On a clean surface, create a mound with the flour. Make a well in the center and crack the eggs into it. Add salt.
- Using a fork, gradually incorporate the flour into the eggs until a dough forms.
- Knead the dough for about 10 minutes until it becomes smooth and elastic.

- Wrap the dough in plastic wrap and let it rest for at least 30 minutes.

Roll Out the Dough:
- Roll out the pasta dough into thin sheets using a pasta machine or a rolling pin.

Assemble the Ravioli:
- Place small portions of the duck filling on one sheet of pasta, leaving space between each portion.
- Lay another sheet of pasta over the top and press around the filling to seal, removing any air bubbles.

Cut and Seal:
- Use a ravioli cutter or a knife to cut out individual ravioli.
- Press the edges firmly to seal the ravioli.

Cook the Ravioli:
- Bring a large pot of salted water to a boil. Cook the ravioli for about 3-4 minutes or until they float to the surface.

For the Sage Brown Butter Sauce:

Brown the Butter:
- In a skillet over medium heat, melt the unsalted butter.
- Add fresh sage leaves to the butter and let them crisp up.

Finish the Sauce:
- Continue cooking the butter until it turns golden brown and has a nutty aroma.
- Season with salt to taste.

Serve:
- Transfer the cooked ravioli to serving plates.
- Spoon the sage brown butter sauce over the ravioli.
- Garnish with chopped fresh parsley and grated Parmesan cheese.

Enjoy your Duck Ravioli with Sage Brown Butter – a rich and flavorful dish perfect for a special occasion or indulgent meal!

Duck and Pineapple Skewers

Ingredients:

For the Marinade:

- 1/4 cup soy sauce
- 2 tablespoons honey
- 2 tablespoons rice vinegar
- 1 tablespoon sesame oil
- 1 tablespoon grated fresh ginger
- 2 cloves garlic, minced
- 1 teaspoon Chinese five-spice powder

For the Skewers:

- 2 duck breasts, boneless and skinless, cut into cubes
- 1 cup fresh pineapple chunks
- Bell peppers, cut into chunks (optional)
- Red onion, cut into chunks (optional)
- Wooden skewers, soaked in water for at least 30 minutes

For Garnish:

- Sesame seeds
- Fresh cilantro, chopped

Instructions:

For the Marinade:

    Prepare the Marinade:
- In a bowl, whisk together soy sauce, honey, rice vinegar, sesame oil, grated ginger, minced garlic, and Chinese five-spice powder.

    Marinate the Duck:
- Place the duck cubes in a shallow dish or a resealable plastic bag.
- Pour the marinade over the duck, ensuring that each piece is well-coated.
- Marinate in the refrigerator for at least 1-2 hours, or overnight for more flavor.

For the Skewers:

Preheat the Grill:
- Preheat your grill or grill pan to medium-high heat.

Assemble the Skewers:
- Thread the marinated duck cubes, pineapple chunks, and any optional vegetables onto the soaked wooden skewers, alternating as desired.

Grill the Skewers:
- Grill the skewers for about 3-4 minutes per side or until the duck is cooked through and has a nice char.

Garnish and Serve:

Garnish:
- Sprinkle sesame seeds and chopped fresh cilantro over the grilled duck and pineapple skewers.

Serve:
- Serve the skewers warm on a platter.

Enjoy these Duck and Pineapple Skewers as a delicious appetizer or main course, with the perfect combination of savory duck and sweet pineapple!

Sesame-Crusted Duck Breast

Ingredients:

For the Duck:

- 2 duck breasts, skin-on
- Salt and black pepper, to taste
- 2 tablespoons soy sauce
- 1 tablespoon honey
- 1 tablespoon rice vinegar
- 1 tablespoon sesame oil

For the Sesame Crust:

- 1/4 cup sesame seeds (white or a mix of white and black)
- 2 tablespoons all-purpose flour
- 1 teaspoon Chinese five-spice powder
- 1/2 teaspoon garlic powder
- 1/2 teaspoon onion powder
- Vegetable oil for searing

For Garnish (Optional):

- Green onions, chopped
- Sesame seeds
- Soy sauce for drizzling

Instructions:

For the Duck:

  Score the Duck Skin:
  - Score the duck skin in a crisscross pattern, being careful not to cut into the meat.

  Marinate the Duck:
  - In a bowl, mix soy sauce, honey, rice vinegar, and sesame oil.
  - Place the duck breasts in a shallow dish and pour the marinade over them. Allow the duck to marinate for at least 30 minutes in the refrigerator.

For the Sesame Crust:

  Combine Crust Ingredients:

- In a bowl, combine sesame seeds, all-purpose flour, Chinese five-spice powder, garlic powder, and onion powder.

Coat the Duck:
- Remove the duck breasts from the marinade and pat them dry with paper towels.
- Press the duck breasts into the sesame crust mixture, coating both sides evenly.

Sear the Duck:
- Heat vegetable oil in an ovenproof skillet over medium-high heat.
- Place the duck breasts in the skillet, skin side down, and sear for about 3-4 minutes until the skin is golden and crispy.
- Flip the duck breasts and sear the other side for an additional 2-3 minutes.

Finish in the Oven:
- Preheat your oven to 375°F (190°C).
- Transfer the skillet to the preheated oven and bake for about 8-10 minutes or until the duck reaches your desired level of doneness.

Serve:

- Allow the sesame-crusted duck breasts to rest for a few minutes before slicing them into thin strips.
- Arrange the slices on a serving plate.
- Garnish with chopped green onions, additional sesame seeds, and a drizzle of soy sauce if desired.

Enjoy your Sesame-Crusted Duck Breast, a dish that combines the rich flavors of duck with the nuttiness of sesame seeds and aromatic spices! Serve it alongside your favorite sides for a delicious meal.

Duck and Roasted Beet Salad

Ingredients:

For the Duck:

- 2 duck breasts, skin-on
- Salt and black pepper, to taste
- 1 tablespoon olive oil

For the Roasted Beets:

- 4 medium-sized beets, peeled and diced
- 2 tablespoons olive oil
- Salt and black pepper, to taste

For the Salad:

- Mixed salad greens (arugula, spinach, or your choice)
- Goat cheese, crumbled
- Candied walnuts or pecans
- Balsamic vinaigrette dressing

Instructions:

For the Duck:

> Prepare the Duck:
> - Score the duck skin in a crisscross pattern. Season both sides of the duck breasts with salt and black pepper.
>
> Sear the Duck:
> - Heat olive oil in a skillet over medium-high heat.
> - Place the duck breasts in the skillet, skin side down, and sear for about 5-7 minutes until the skin is golden and crispy.
> - Flip the duck breasts and sear the other side for an additional 2-3 minutes.
> - Transfer the duck to a cutting board and let it rest for a few minutes before slicing it into thin strips.

For the Roasted Beets:

> Preheat the Oven:
> - Preheat your oven to 400°F (200°C).

Prepare the Beets:
- In a bowl, toss the diced beets with olive oil, salt, and black pepper.

Roast the Beets:
- Spread the beets on a baking sheet in a single layer.
- Roast in the preheated oven for about 25-30 minutes or until the beets are tender and caramelized. Stir occasionally for even cooking.

Assemble the Salad:

Combine Ingredients:
- In a large salad bowl, combine the mixed salad greens, crumbled goat cheese, candied walnuts or pecans, and the roasted beets.

Add Sliced Duck:
- Arrange the sliced duck on top of the salad.

Drizzle with Dressing:
- Drizzle balsamic vinaigrette dressing over the salad.

Toss Gently:
- Gently toss the salad to combine all the ingredients.

Serve:
- Serve the Duck and Roasted Beet Salad on individual plates.

Enjoy this delightful salad with the perfect combination of succulent duck, earthy roasted beets, creamy goat cheese, and crunchy candied nuts!

Duck and Apricot Compote

Ingredients:

For the Duck:

- 2 duck breasts, skin-on
- Salt and black pepper, to taste
- 1 tablespoon olive oil

For the Apricot Compote:

- 1 cup dried apricots, chopped
- 1/2 cup orange juice
- 1/4 cup water
- 2 tablespoons honey
- 1 teaspoon fresh ginger, grated
- 1/2 teaspoon cinnamon
- 1/4 teaspoon nutmeg
- 1/4 cup chopped pistachios (for garnish)

Instructions:

For the Duck:

    Prepare the Duck:
- Score the duck skin in a crisscross pattern. Season both sides of the duck breasts with salt and black pepper.

    Sear the Duck:
- Heat olive oil in a skillet over medium-high heat.
- Place the duck breasts in the skillet, skin side down, and sear for about 5-7 minutes until the skin is golden and crispy.
- Flip the duck breasts and sear the other side for an additional 2-3 minutes.
- Transfer the duck to a cutting board and let it rest for a few minutes before slicing it into thin strips.

For the Apricot Compote:

    Prepare the Compote:
- In a saucepan, combine chopped dried apricots, orange juice, water, honey, grated ginger, cinnamon, and nutmeg.

    Simmer:

- Bring the mixture to a simmer over medium heat.

Cook Down:
- Reduce the heat to low and let it simmer for about 15-20 minutes, or until the apricots are soft and the compote thickens.

Adjust Sweetness:
- Taste the compote and adjust the sweetness by adding more honey if needed.

Serve:

- Arrange the sliced duck on a serving plate.
- Spoon the Apricot Compote over the duck.
- Garnish with chopped pistachios.

Enjoy your Duck with Apricot Compote, a delightful combination of savory duck with the sweet and tangy flavors of the apricot compote! Serve it with your favorite side dishes for a delicious and elegant meal.

Duck Ramen Bowl

Ingredients:

For the Duck:

- 2 duck breasts, skin-on
- Salt and black pepper, to taste
- 1 tablespoon soy sauce
- 1 tablespoon hoisin sauce
- 1 tablespoon mirin
- 1 tablespoon sesame oil
- 2 cloves garlic, minced
- 1 teaspoon fresh ginger, grated

For the Ramen Bowl:

- 4 packs of ramen noodles (discard seasoning packets)
- 6 cups chicken or duck broth
- 2 tablespoons soy sauce
- 1 tablespoon miso paste
- 1 tablespoon sesame oil
- 1 cup shiitake mushrooms, sliced
- 1 cup baby bok choy, chopped
- 2 boiled eggs, halved
- Green onions, sliced (for garnish)
- Sesame seeds (for garnish)

Instructions:

For the Duck:

    Prepare the Duck:
- Score the duck skin in a crisscross pattern. Season both sides with salt and black pepper.

    Marinate the Duck:
- In a bowl, mix soy sauce, hoisin sauce, mirin, sesame oil, minced garlic, and grated ginger.
- Coat the duck breasts with the marinade and let them marinate for at least 30 minutes.

    Cook the Duck:
- Preheat the oven to 400°F (200°C).

- Heat an oven-safe skillet over medium-high heat.
- Sear the duck breasts, skin side down, for about 3-4 minutes until the skin is golden brown.
- Flip the duck breasts and transfer the skillet to the preheated oven.
- Roast for 12-15 minutes or until the duck is cooked to your liking.
- Let the duck rest for a few minutes before slicing it thinly.

For the Ramen Bowl:

Prepare Ramen Noodles:
- Cook the ramen noodles according to package instructions. Drain and set aside.

Make the Broth:
- In a large pot, heat chicken or duck broth over medium heat.
- Add soy sauce, miso paste, and sesame oil. Stir until the miso paste is fully dissolved.

Add Vegetables:
- Add sliced shiitake mushrooms and chopped baby bok choy to the broth. Simmer until the vegetables are tender.

Assemble the Bowl:
- Divide the cooked ramen noodles among serving bowls.
- Pour the hot broth over the noodles and add slices of the cooked duck on top.

Garnish:
- Garnish the ramen bowls with halved boiled eggs, sliced green onions, and sesame seeds.

Enjoy your Duck Ramen Bowl, a comforting and flavorful dish with rich broth and tender duck slices!

Orange-Chipotle Glazed Duck Drumsticks

Ingredients:

For the Duck Drumsticks:

- 8 duck drumsticks
- Salt and black pepper, to taste
- 1 tablespoon olive oil

For the Orange-Chipotle Glaze:

- Zest and juice of 2 oranges
- 2 chipotle peppers in adobo sauce, minced
- 1/4 cup honey
- 2 tablespoons soy sauce
- 1 tablespoon Dijon mustard
- 1 teaspoon ground cumin
- 1 teaspoon smoked paprika

For Garnish:

- Fresh cilantro, chopped
- Orange slices

Instructions:

For the Duck Drumsticks:

> Preheat the Oven:
> - Preheat your oven to 400°F (200°C).
>
> Season the Drumsticks:
> - Pat the duck drumsticks dry with paper towels. Season with salt and black pepper.
>
> Sear the Drumsticks:
> - Heat olive oil in an oven-safe skillet over medium-high heat.
> - Sear the duck drumsticks until browned on all sides, about 5 minutes.
>
> Prepare the Glaze:
> - In a bowl, whisk together the orange zest, orange juice, minced chipotle peppers, honey, soy sauce, Dijon mustard, ground cumin, and smoked paprika.
>
> Glaze the Drumsticks:
> - Brush the duck drumsticks with the prepared orange-chipotle glaze.

Bake:
- Transfer the skillet to the preheated oven and bake for about 30-35 minutes or until the duck is cooked through and the skin is crispy. Baste the drumsticks with the glaze during baking.

Serve:

- Arrange the Orange-Chipotle Glazed Duck Drumsticks on a serving platter.
- Drizzle with any remaining glaze.
- Garnish with chopped fresh cilantro and orange slices.

Enjoy these flavorful and slightly spicy Orange-Chipotle Glazed Duck Drumsticks! They make a delicious and impressive dish for any occasion.

Duck and Sweet Potato Hash

Ingredients:

- 2 duck breasts, cooked and shredded
- 2 large sweet potatoes, peeled and diced into small cubes
- 1 onion, finely chopped
- 2 cloves garlic, minced
- 1 bell pepper, diced
- 2 tablespoons olive oil
- 1 teaspoon smoked paprika
- 1 teaspoon dried thyme
- Salt and black pepper, to taste
- Fresh parsley, chopped (for garnish)
- Poached or fried eggs (optional, for serving)

Instructions:

Cook the Duck:
- If not already cooked, season duck breasts with salt and black pepper. Sear in a hot skillet, skin side down, until crispy. Flip and cook until desired doneness. Shred the duck meat and set aside.

Prepare Sweet Potatoes:
- In a large skillet, heat olive oil over medium heat. Add diced sweet potatoes and cook until they start to soften and turn golden brown.

Add Vegetables:
- Add chopped onion, minced garlic, and diced bell pepper to the skillet. Sauté until the vegetables are tender.

Season and Spice:
- Sprinkle smoked paprika, dried thyme, salt, and black pepper over the sweet potato mixture. Stir to combine.

Incorporate Duck:
- Add the shredded duck to the skillet. Mix well, allowing the flavors to meld.

Cook until Crispy:
- Allow the hash to cook for a few minutes, stirring occasionally, until the sweet potatoes are crispy and golden brown.

Garnish:
- Garnish the Duck and Sweet Potato Hash with chopped fresh parsley.

Serve with Eggs (Optional):
- Optionally, serve the hash with poached or fried eggs on top.

Enjoy your Duck and Sweet Potato Hash as a hearty and flavorful breakfast or brunch dish!

Duck and Mango Salsa

Ingredients:

For the Duck:

- 2 duck breasts, skin-on
- Salt and black pepper, to taste
- 1 tablespoon olive oil

For the Mango Salsa:

- 2 ripe mangoes, peeled and diced
- 1/2 red onion, finely chopped
- 1 red bell pepper, diced
- 1 jalapeño, seeds removed and finely chopped
- Juice of 1 lime
- 2 tablespoons fresh cilantro, chopped
- Salt and black pepper, to taste

Instructions:

For the Duck:

    Prepare the Duck:
- Score the duck skin in a crisscross pattern. Season both sides of the duck breasts with salt and black pepper.

    Sear the Duck:
- Heat olive oil in a skillet over medium-high heat.
- Place the duck breasts in the skillet, skin side down, and sear for about 5-7 minutes until the skin is golden and crispy.
- Flip the duck breasts and sear the other side for an additional 2-3 minutes.
- Transfer the duck to a cutting board and let it rest for a few minutes before slicing it into thin strips.

For the Mango Salsa:

    Prepare the Mango Salsa:
- In a bowl, combine diced mangoes, finely chopped red onion, diced red bell pepper, chopped jalapeño, lime juice, and chopped cilantro.

    Season the Salsa:
- Season the salsa with salt and black pepper. Adjust the seasoning to your taste.

Serve:

- Arrange the sliced duck on a serving plate.
- Spoon the Mango Salsa over the duck slices.

Enjoy your Duck with Mango Salsa, a delightful combination of savory duck with the sweetness and freshness of mango salsa! This dish is perfect for a light and flavorful meal.

Duck and Spinach Stuffed Shells

Ingredients:

For the Duck and Spinach Filling:

- 1 pound ground duck meat
- 1 tablespoon olive oil
- 1 onion, finely chopped
- 2 cloves garlic, minced
- 1 cup fresh spinach, chopped
- Salt and black pepper, to taste
- 1 teaspoon dried oregano
- 1 teaspoon dried basil
- 1 cup ricotta cheese
- 1/2 cup grated Parmesan cheese
- 1 egg

For the Sauce:

- 2 cups marinara sauce
- 1 teaspoon dried Italian herbs (oregano, basil, thyme)
- Salt and black pepper, to taste

For the Stuffed Shells:

- 1 box (12-16 ounces) jumbo pasta shells, cooked according to package instructions
- 1 1/2 cups shredded mozzarella cheese
- Fresh parsley, chopped (for garnish)

Instructions:

For the Duck and Spinach Filling:

   Cook Duck:
- In a skillet, heat olive oil over medium heat. Add chopped onion and minced garlic, sauté until softened.
- Add ground duck meat and cook until browned. Drain excess fat.

   Add Spinach:
- Stir in chopped spinach and cook until wilted.

Season:
- Season the duck mixture with salt, black pepper, dried oregano, and dried basil. Mix well.

Prepare Filling Mixture:
- In a bowl, combine the cooked duck mixture with ricotta cheese, grated Parmesan cheese, and the egg. Mix until well combined.

For the Sauce:

Combine Ingredients:
- In a saucepan, mix marinara sauce with dried Italian herbs, salt, and black pepper. Simmer over low heat.

For the Stuffed Shells:

Preheat Oven:
- Preheat your oven to 375°F (190°C).

Stuff Shells:
- Spoon the duck and spinach filling into the cooked jumbo pasta shells.

Assemble:
- Spread a thin layer of the marinara sauce at the bottom of a baking dish.
- Arrange the stuffed shells in the dish.

Cover with Sauce:
- Pour the remaining marinara sauce over the stuffed shells, ensuring they are well-covered.

Add Cheese:
- Sprinkle shredded mozzarella cheese over the top.

Bake:
- Cover the baking dish with foil and bake in the preheated oven for 20-25 minutes, or until the cheese is melted and bubbly.

Finish and Serve:
- Remove the foil and bake for an additional 5-10 minutes until the cheese is golden brown.
- Garnish with chopped fresh parsley before serving.

Enjoy your Duck and Spinach Stuffed Shells, a delightful combination of rich duck, flavorful spinach, and gooey cheese! Serve it with a side salad for a complete meal.

Five-Spice Duck Lettuce Wraps

Ingredients:

For the Five-Spice Duck:

- 2 duck breasts, skin-on
- 2 tablespoons soy sauce
- 1 tablespoon hoisin sauce
- 1 tablespoon oyster sauce
- 1 tablespoon honey
- 1 teaspoon Chinese five-spice powder
- 2 cloves garlic, minced
- 1 tablespoon sesame oil
- Salt and black pepper, to taste

For the Lettuce Wraps:

- Large lettuce leaves (iceberg or butter lettuce)
- 1 cup cooked rice noodles (optional)
- 1 cup julienned vegetables (carrots, bell peppers, cucumber)
- Fresh herbs (cilantro, mint, basil), chopped
- Green onions, sliced
- Crushed peanuts (optional)
- Lime wedges (for serving)

Instructions:

For the Five-Spice Duck:

Prepare Duck Marinade:
- In a bowl, whisk together soy sauce, hoisin sauce, oyster sauce, honey, Chinese five-spice powder, minced garlic, sesame oil, salt, and black pepper.

Marinate Duck:
- Place the duck breasts in a shallow dish and pour the marinade over them. Ensure the duck is well coated. Marinate for at least 30 minutes or longer for more flavor.

Cook Duck:
- Preheat the oven to 400°F (200°C).
- Heat an oven-safe skillet over medium-high heat. Sear the duck breasts, skin side down, for 3-4 minutes until the skin is golden brown.

- Flip the duck and transfer the skillet to the preheated oven. Roast for about 10-12 minutes or until the duck is cooked to your liking.
- Let the duck rest for a few minutes before slicing it thinly.

For the Lettuce Wraps:

Assemble Wraps:
- Lay out large lettuce leaves on a serving platter.
- If using, place a small amount of cooked rice noodles in each lettuce leaf.

Add Duck and Vegetables:
- Top with slices of the five-spice duck.
- Add julienned vegetables, chopped fresh herbs, and sliced green onions on top.

Optional Toppings:
- Sprinkle crushed peanuts on top for added crunch.

Serve:
- Serve the Five-Spice Duck Lettuce Wraps with lime wedges on the side.

Enjoy these flavorful and refreshing Five-Spice Duck Lettuce Wraps as a light and satisfying meal!

Duck and Blue Cheese Flatbread

Ingredients:

For the Duck:

- 2 duck breasts, skin-on
- Salt and black pepper, to taste
- 1 tablespoon olive oil
- 2 tablespoons balsamic vinegar
- 2 tablespoons honey
- 1 teaspoon Dijon mustard

For the Flatbread:

- 1 pre-made flatbread or pizza crust
- 1 cup caramelized onions
- 1 cup cooked and shredded duck meat (from the prepared duck breasts)
- 1/2 cup crumbled blue cheese
- Fresh thyme leaves, for garnish

Instructions:

For the Duck:

    Prepare Duck:
- Score the duck skin in a crisscross pattern. Season both sides of the duck breasts with salt and black pepper.

    Sear Duck:
- Heat olive oil in a skillet over medium-high heat. Sear the duck breasts, skin side down, for 3-4 minutes until the skin is golden brown.

    Flip and Cook:
- Flip the duck breasts and cook the other side for an additional 2-3 minutes.

    Make Glaze:
- In a small bowl, mix balsamic vinegar, honey, and Dijon mustard. Pour the glaze over the duck breasts and cook for another 2-3 minutes until the glaze thickens.

    Slice Duck:
- Let the duck rest for a few minutes before slicing it thinly.

For the Flatbread:

- Preheat Oven:
  - Preheat your oven to the temperature recommended for the flatbread or pizza crust.
- Assemble Flatbread:
  - Spread the caramelized onions evenly over the flatbread.
- Add Duck and Blue Cheese:
  - Scatter the shredded duck meat over the onions.
  - Sprinkle crumbled blue cheese evenly across the flatbread.
- Bake:
  - Place the flatbread on a baking sheet or pizza stone and bake according to the package instructions or until the cheese is melted and bubbly.
- Finish and Garnish:
  - Once out of the oven, arrange the sliced duck on top and garnish with fresh thyme leaves.
- Slice and Serve:
  - Slice the Duck and Blue Cheese Flatbread into wedges and serve.

Enjoy this Duck and Blue Cheese Flatbread with its combination of rich duck, tangy blue cheese, and sweet balsamic glaze! It makes for a delightful appetizer or main dish.

Duck and Cranberry Puff Pastry Bites

Ingredients:

For the Duck:

- 2 duck breasts, skin-on
- Salt and black pepper, to taste
- 1 tablespoon olive oil

For the Cranberry Sauce:

- 1 cup fresh or frozen cranberries
- 1/2 cup sugar
- 1/4 cup water
- Zest and juice of 1 orange

For the Puff Pastry Bites:

- 1 sheet puff pastry, thawed if frozen
- 1 egg, beaten (for egg wash)
- 1/2 cup crumbled goat cheese or blue cheese (optional)
- Fresh thyme leaves, for garnish

Instructions:

For the Duck:

> Prepare Duck:
> - Score the duck skin in a crisscross pattern. Season both sides of the duck breasts with salt and black pepper.
>
> Sear Duck:
> - Heat olive oil in a skillet over medium-high heat. Sear the duck breasts, skin side down, for 3-4 minutes until the skin is golden brown.
>
> Flip and Cook:
> - Flip the duck breasts and cook the other side for an additional 2-3 minutes.
>
> Slice Duck:
> - Let the duck rest for a few minutes before slicing it thinly.

For the Cranberry Sauce:

> Cook Cranberries:
> - In a saucepan, combine cranberries, sugar, water, orange zest, and orange juice.

Simmer:
- Bring the mixture to a simmer over medium heat.

Cook Down:
- Reduce the heat to low and let it simmer for about 10-15 minutes, or until the cranberries have burst and the sauce has thickened.

Cool:
- Allow the cranberry sauce to cool before using.

For the Puff Pastry Bites:

Preheat Oven:
- Preheat your oven to 400°F (200°C).

Roll Out Puff Pastry:
- Roll out the puff pastry sheet on a floured surface. Cut it into small squares or circles.

Assemble Bites:
- Place a small amount of cranberry sauce on each pastry square.
- Top with a slice of seared duck.
- If desired, add a small amount of crumbled goat cheese or blue cheese on top.

Fold and Seal:
- Fold the pastry over the filling and seal the edges. Brush with beaten egg for a golden finish.

Bake:
- Place the assembled puff pastry bites on a baking sheet and bake in the preheated oven for 15-20 minutes, or until the pastry is golden brown and puffed.

Garnish:
- Garnish with fresh thyme leaves before serving.

Enjoy these Duck and Cranberry Puff Pastry Bites as a delightful appetizer or party snack with a perfect balance of flavors!

Duck and Asparagus Quiche

Ingredients:

For the Quiche Filling:

- 1 pre-made pie crust or puff pastry, thawed
- 1 cup cooked and shredded duck meat
- 1 cup asparagus spears, trimmed and chopped
- 1 cup shredded Gruyere or Swiss cheese
- 1/2 cup cherry tomatoes, halved
- 4 large eggs
- 1 cup whole milk
- 1/2 cup heavy cream
- Salt and black pepper, to taste
- 1/2 teaspoon dried thyme
- 1/4 teaspoon ground nutmeg

Instructions:

Preheat Oven:
- Preheat your oven to 375°F (190°C).

Prepare Crust:
- Roll out the pie crust or puff pastry and line a quiche or pie dish. Trim any excess crust.

Blind Bake (Optional):
- If using puff pastry, you may blind bake it by placing parchment paper over the crust and adding pie weights or dried beans. Bake for about 10 minutes to set the crust slightly. Remove weights and parchment.

Prepare Filling:
- In a bowl, whisk together eggs, whole milk, heavy cream, salt, black pepper, dried thyme, and ground nutmeg.

Assemble Quiche:
- Spread shredded duck meat, chopped asparagus, cherry tomato halves, and shredded cheese evenly over the pie crust.

Pour Egg Mixture:
- Pour the egg mixture over the filling ingredients in the pie crust.

Bake:
- Bake in the preheated oven for 35-40 minutes or until the quiche is set and the top is golden brown.

Cool and Slice:
- Allow the quiche to cool for a few minutes before slicing.

Serve:
- Serve the Duck and Asparagus Quiche warm.

Enjoy this delicious Duck and Asparagus Quiche, perfect for brunch or a light dinner! Customize it with your favorite herbs and cheeses for added flavor.

BBQ Pulled Duck Sliders

Ingredients:

For the Pulled Duck:

- 2 duck leg quarters
- Salt and black pepper, to taste
- 1 teaspoon smoked paprika
- 1 teaspoon garlic powder
- 1 teaspoon onion powder
- 1/2 teaspoon cayenne pepper
- 1 cup barbecue sauce

For the Sliders:

- Mini slider buns
- Coleslaw (store-bought or homemade)
- Pickles, sliced (optional, for topping)

Instructions:

For the Pulled Duck:

    Preheat Oven:
- Preheat your oven to 325°F (163°C).

    Season Duck Legs:
- Season the duck leg quarters with salt, black pepper, smoked paprika, garlic powder, onion powder, and cayenne pepper.

    Sear Duck Legs:
- Heat a skillet over medium-high heat. Sear the duck leg quarters, skin side down, until the skin is golden brown.

    Braise in BBQ Sauce:
- Transfer the seared duck legs to a baking dish. Pour barbecue sauce over the duck legs, ensuring they are well coated.
- Cover the baking dish with foil and bake in the preheated oven for 2 to 2.5 hours or until the duck is tender and easily shreds.

    Shred Duck:
- Remove the duck from the oven and let it cool slightly. Shred the duck meat using two forks, discarding the bones and skin.

    Mix with BBQ Sauce:

- Mix the shredded duck with additional barbecue sauce for extra flavor and moisture.

For Assembling Sliders:

    Prepare Slider Buns:
- Toast the mini slider buns in the oven or on a skillet for a minute or two until they are lightly golden.

    Assemble Sliders:
- Place a spoonful of the pulled duck on the bottom half of each slider bun.

    Add Coleslaw:
- Top the pulled duck with a layer of coleslaw.

    Optional Toppings:
- Add sliced pickles on top, if desired.

    Top with Bun:
- Place the top half of the slider bun over the coleslaw to complete the slider.

    Serve:
- Serve the BBQ Pulled Duck Sliders warm.

These BBQ Pulled Duck Sliders make for a delicious and satisfying appetizer or party snack. Enjoy the combination of tender pulled duck, tangy barbecue sauce, and refreshing coleslaw!

Duck and Roasted Garlic Mashed Potatoes

Ingredients:

For the Duck:

- 2 duck breasts, skin-on
- Salt and black pepper, to taste
- 1 tablespoon olive oil
- 4 cloves garlic, minced
- 1 teaspoon fresh rosemary, chopped

For the Roasted Garlic Mashed Potatoes:

- 4 large russet potatoes, peeled and cut into chunks
- 1 head of garlic
- 1/2 cup unsalted butter
- 1/2 cup milk (or cream)
- Salt and black pepper, to taste
- Chives, chopped (for garnish)

Instructions:

For the Duck:

Preheat Oven:
- Preheat your oven to 400°F (200°C).

Season Duck:
- Score the duck skin in a crisscross pattern. Season both sides of the duck breasts with salt and black pepper.

Sear Duck:
- Heat olive oil in an oven-safe skillet over medium-high heat. Sear the duck breasts, skin side down, for 3-4 minutes until the skin is golden brown.

Add Aromatics:
- Flip the duck breasts. Add minced garlic and chopped rosemary to the skillet. Cook for an additional 2-3 minutes.

Roast Duck:
- Transfer the skillet to the preheated oven and roast for about 10-12 minutes or until the duck is cooked to your liking.

Slice Duck:
- Let the duck rest for a few minutes before slicing it thinly.

For the Roasted Garlic Mashed Potatoes:

- Roast Garlic:
  - Cut the top off the head of garlic to expose the cloves. Drizzle with olive oil, wrap in foil, and roast in the oven for about 30-40 minutes or until the garlic is soft and golden.
- Boil Potatoes:
  - Boil the peeled and chopped potatoes in salted water until tender. Drain.
- Prepare Mashed Potatoes:
  - In a large bowl, mash the boiled potatoes. Squeeze the roasted garlic cloves into the mashed potatoes.
- Add Butter and Milk:
  - Add butter and milk (or cream) to the mashed potatoes. Mash and mix until smooth.
- Season:
  - Season the mashed potatoes with salt and black pepper to taste.

Serve:

- Serve the sliced Duck over a generous serving of Roasted Garlic Mashed Potatoes.
- Garnish with chopped chives.

Enjoy this comforting and flavorful dish of Duck and Roasted Garlic Mashed Potatoes! The rich and tender duck complements the creamy and garlicky mashed potatoes perfectly.

Duck and Lemon Risotto

Ingredients:

For the Duck:

- 2 duck breasts, skin-on
- Salt and black pepper, to taste
- 1 tablespoon olive oil
- Zest of 1 lemon
- Juice of 1 lemon

For the Risotto:

- 1 1/2 cups Arborio rice
- 1/2 cup dry white wine
- 4 cups chicken or vegetable broth, kept warm
- 1 small onion, finely chopped
- 2 cloves garlic, minced
- 1/2 cup Parmesan cheese, grated
- 2 tablespoons unsalted butter
- Fresh parsley, chopped (for garnish)
- Salt and black pepper, to taste

Instructions:

For the Duck:

   Preheat Oven:
   - Preheat your oven to 400°F (200°C).

   Season Duck:
   - Score the duck skin in a crisscross pattern. Season both sides of the duck breasts with salt and black pepper.

   Sear Duck:
   - Heat olive oil in an oven-safe skillet over medium-high heat. Sear the duck breasts, skin side down, for 3-4 minutes until the skin is golden brown.

   Add Lemon Zest and Juice:
   - Flip the duck breasts. Add lemon zest and juice to the skillet. Cook for an additional 2-3 minutes.

   Roast Duck:

- Transfer the skillet to the preheated oven and roast for about 10-12 minutes or until the duck is cooked to your liking.

Slice Duck:
- Let the duck rest for a few minutes before slicing it thinly.

For the Risotto:

Saute Onion and Garlic:
- In a separate large pan, heat a bit of olive oil over medium heat. Add chopped onion and sauté until softened. Add minced garlic and cook for another 1-2 minutes.

Toast Rice:
- Add Arborio rice to the pan and cook, stirring, until the rice is lightly toasted.

Deglaze with Wine:
- Pour in the white wine to deglaze the pan, stirring constantly until the wine is mostly absorbed.

Add Broth:
- Begin adding the warm broth, one ladle at a time, stirring continuously. Allow the liquid to be absorbed before adding the next ladle. Continue this process until the rice is creamy and cooked to al dente.

Finish Risotto:
- Stir in grated Parmesan cheese and butter until melted and well combined. Season with salt and black pepper to taste.

Serve:
- Serve the Duck slices over a generous portion of Lemon Risotto.
- Garnish with chopped fresh parsley.

Enjoy the bright and zesty flavors of Duck and Lemon Risotto! The creamy risotto pairs wonderfully with the tender and citrus-infused duck.

Duck and Portobello Mushroom Pizza

Ingredients:

For the Pizza:

- 1 pre-made pizza crust or pizza dough
- 1 cup cooked and shredded duck meat
- 1 cup sliced Portobello mushrooms
- 1 cup shredded mozzarella cheese
- 1/2 cup crumbled goat cheese
- 2 tablespoons balsamic glaze (for drizzling)
- Fresh thyme leaves (for garnish)

For the Duck:

- 2 duck breasts, skin-on
- Salt and black pepper, to taste
- 1 tablespoon olive oil

Instructions:

For the Duck:

> Preheat Oven:
> - Preheat your oven to 400°F (200°C).
>
> Season Duck:
> - Score the duck skin in a crisscross pattern. Season both sides of the duck breasts with salt and black pepper.
>
> Sear Duck:
> - Heat olive oil in an oven-safe skillet over medium-high heat. Sear the duck breasts, skin side down, for 3-4 minutes until the skin is golden brown.
>
> Finish in Oven:
> - Flip the duck breasts. Transfer the skillet to the preheated oven and roast for about 10-12 minutes or until the duck is cooked to your liking.
>
> Slice Duck:
> - Let the duck rest for a few minutes before slicing it thinly.

For the Pizza:

> Preheat Oven:

- Preheat your oven according to the pizza crust or dough package instructions.

Assemble Pizza:
- Roll out the pizza dough or use a pre-made pizza crust.
- Spread a thin layer of olive oil on the crust.

Add Toppings:
- Evenly distribute shredded duck, sliced Portobello mushrooms, mozzarella cheese, and crumbled goat cheese over the pizza.

Bake:
- Bake the pizza in the preheated oven according to the pizza crust or dough package instructions, usually around 12-15 minutes or until the crust is golden and the cheese is melted and bubbly.

Finish and Serve:
- Once out of the oven, drizzle balsamic glaze over the pizza.
- Garnish with fresh thyme leaves.

Slice and Enjoy:
- Slice the Duck and Portobello Mushroom Pizza and serve hot.

Enjoy this gourmet pizza with the rich flavors of duck, earthy Portobello mushrooms, and tangy goat cheese!

Smoked Duck and Gouda Quesadillas

Ingredients:

- 2 duck breasts, smoked and shredded
- 1 cup Gouda cheese, shredded
- 1 cup Monterey Jack cheese, shredded
- 1/2 cup red onion, finely chopped
- 1/4 cup fresh cilantro, chopped
- 4 large flour tortillas
- Olive oil or butter (for cooking)
- Sour cream (for serving)
- Salsa (for serving)

Instructions:

Prepare Smoked Duck:
- Smoke the duck breasts according to your preferred method. Once smoked, shred the duck meat.

Assemble Quesadillas:
- Place one tortilla on a clean surface. Sprinkle a layer of Gouda and Monterey Jack cheese on one half of the tortilla.
- Add a portion of shredded smoked duck on top of the cheese.
- Sprinkle chopped red onion and fresh cilantro over the duck.
- Top with another layer of cheese.

Fold and Press:
- Fold the tortilla in half to cover the filling, creating a half-moon shape.
- Press the edges gently to seal the quesadilla.

Cook Quesadillas:
- Heat a skillet or griddle over medium heat. Add a drizzle of olive oil or a small amount of butter.
- Place the assembled quesadilla on the skillet and cook for 3-4 minutes per side or until the tortilla is golden brown and the cheese is melted.

Repeat:
- Repeat the process for the remaining tortillas and filling.

Slice and Serve:
- Once cooked, transfer the quesadillas to a cutting board and let them rest for a minute before slicing into wedges.

Serve with Sour Cream and Salsa:

- Serve the smoked duck and Gouda quesadillas with a side of sour cream and salsa.

Enjoy these Smoked Duck and Gouda Quesadillas as a flavorful and satisfying appetizer or main dish!

Duck and Caramelized Onion Tart

Ingredients:

For the Tart:

- 1 sheet puff pastry, thawed
- 2 duck breasts, cooked and shredded
- 2 large onions, thinly sliced
- 2 tablespoons olive oil
- 1 tablespoon balsamic vinegar
- 1 tablespoon honey
- Salt and black pepper, to taste
- 1 cup Gruyere or Swiss cheese, shredded
- Fresh thyme leaves, for garnish

For the Balsamic Reduction:

- 1/2 cup balsamic vinegar
- 2 tablespoons brown sugar

Instructions:

For the Tart:

Preheat Oven:
- Preheat your oven to 400°F (200°C).

Caramelize Onions:
- In a skillet, heat olive oil over medium heat. Add thinly sliced onions and cook, stirring occasionally, until they are soft and caramelized.
- Stir in balsamic vinegar and honey, and continue to cook for an additional 5-7 minutes until the onions are deeply caramelized. Season with salt and black pepper.

Prepare Puff Pastry:
- Roll out the puff pastry sheet on a lightly floured surface. Place it on a baking sheet lined with parchment paper.

Assemble Tart:
- Spread the caramelized onions evenly over the puff pastry, leaving a border around the edges.
- Distribute the shredded duck evenly over the caramelized onions.
- Sprinkle shredded Gruyere or Swiss cheese over the top.

Bake:

- Bake in the preheated oven for 20-25 minutes or until the puff pastry is golden brown and the cheese is melted and bubbly.

Garnish:
- Remove the tart from the oven and let it cool for a few minutes. Garnish with fresh thyme leaves.

For the Balsamic Reduction:

Make Balsamic Reduction:
- In a small saucepan, combine balsamic vinegar and brown sugar. Bring to a simmer over medium heat.
- Cook, stirring occasionally, until the mixture has reduced by half and has a syrupy consistency.

Drizzle Over Tart:
- Drizzle the balsamic reduction over the duck and caramelized onion tart.

Slice and Serve:
- Slice the tart into squares or wedges and serve warm.

Enjoy this Duck and Caramelized Onion Tart with its perfect combination of savory duck, sweet caramelized onions, and rich balsamic reduction!

Duck and Apple Slaw

Ingredients:

For the Duck:

- 2 duck breasts, cooked and thinly sliced
- Salt and black pepper, to taste
- 1 tablespoon olive oil
- 2 tablespoons honey

For the Apple Slaw:

- 2 apples, julienned (use a mix of sweet and tart varieties)
- 1 cup red cabbage, thinly sliced
- 1 cup green cabbage, thinly sliced
- 1 carrot, julienned
- 1/2 cup red onion, thinly sliced
- 1/4 cup fresh parsley, chopped

For the Dressing:

- 3 tablespoons apple cider vinegar
- 2 tablespoons olive oil
- 1 tablespoon Dijon mustard
- 1 tablespoon honey
- Salt and black pepper, to taste

Instructions:

For the Duck:

> Preheat Pan:
> - Preheat a skillet over medium-high heat.
>
> Season Duck:
> - Season duck breasts with salt and black pepper.
>
> Sear Duck:
> - Add olive oil to the hot skillet. Sear the duck breasts, skin side down, for 3-4 minutes until the skin is crispy. Flip and cook for an additional 2-3 minutes.
>
> Brush with Honey:
> - Brush the duck breasts with honey during the last minute of cooking. Let them rest for a few minutes before slicing thinly.

For the Apple Slaw:

- Prepare Ingredients:
  - In a large bowl, combine julienned apples, sliced red cabbage, sliced green cabbage, julienned carrot, sliced red onion, and chopped parsley.
- Make Dressing:
  - In a small bowl, whisk together apple cider vinegar, olive oil, Dijon mustard, honey, salt, and black pepper.
- Combine:
  - Pour the dressing over the apple and vegetable mixture. Toss until everything is well coated.

Assemble Duck and Apple Slaw:

- Plate Slaw:
  - Arrange a generous portion of the apple slaw on individual plates or a serving platter.
- Top with Duck:
  - Place slices of the honey-glazed duck on top of the apple slaw.
- Garnish:
  - Garnish with additional parsley if desired.
- Serve:
  - Serve the Duck and Apple Slaw immediately, and enjoy the crispiness of the slaw combined with the succulent duck.

This Duck and Apple Slaw is a delightful blend of sweet and savory flavors, making it a perfect light and refreshing dish!

Ginger-Soy Glazed Duck Breast

Ingredients:

For the Duck:

- 2 duck breasts, skin-on
- Salt and black pepper, to taste
- 2 tablespoons soy sauce
- 1 tablespoon ginger, grated
- 2 tablespoons honey
- 1 tablespoon rice vinegar
- 2 cloves garlic, minced
- 1 tablespoon sesame oil (for searing)

For Garnish:

- Green onions, sliced
- Sesame seeds
- Fresh cilantro, chopped

Instructions:

Preheat Oven:
- Preheat your oven to 375°F (190°C).

Score Duck Skin:
- Using a sharp knife, score the duck skin in a crisscross pattern, being careful not to cut into the meat.

Season Duck:
- Season the duck breasts with salt and black pepper.

Prepare Glaze:
- In a small bowl, whisk together soy sauce, grated ginger, honey, rice vinegar, and minced garlic to create the ginger-soy glaze.

Marinate Duck:
- Brush the duck breasts with the ginger-soy glaze, ensuring they are well coated. Allow them to marinate for at least 15-20 minutes.

Sear Duck:
- Heat sesame oil in an oven-safe skillet over medium-high heat. Place the duck breasts, skin side down, and sear for 3-4 minutes until the skin is golden brown.

Glaze Duck:
- Flip the duck breasts and brush the top side with more of the ginger-soy glaze.

Roast in Oven:
- Transfer the skillet to the preheated oven and roast for about 12-15 minutes or until the duck is cooked to your liking.

Baste:
- Baste the duck with the glaze every 5 minutes during the roasting process.

Rest and Slice:
- Let the duck rest for a few minutes before slicing it thinly.

Garnish:
- Garnish the sliced duck with green onions, sesame seeds, and chopped cilantro.

Serve:
- Serve the Ginger-Soy Glazed Duck Breast slices on a platter or individual plates.

Enjoy this Ginger-Soy Glazed Duck Breast, where the rich and flavorful duck is complemented by the savory-sweet and aromatic ginger-soy glaze!

www.ingramcontent.com/pod-product-compliance
Lightning Source LLC
LaVergne TN
LVHW081558060526
838201LV00054B/1944